DADDY DEVOS TODAY

DADDY DEVOS TODAY

A Father's Heart Expressed in Text, 160 Characters or Less, Every Day!

JOHN MICHIELI

LUCIDBOOKS

Daddy Devos Today

Copyright © 2012 by John Michieli

Published by Lucid Books in Brenham, TX.
www.LucidBooks.net

All rights reserved. No part of this publication may be reproduced, stored in a retrieval system, or transmitted in any form by any means, electronic, mechanical, photocopy, recording, or otherwise, without the prior permission of the publisher, except as provided for by USA copyright law.

First Printing 2012

ISBN-13: 9781935909170
ISBN-10: 1-935909-17-7

Scripture quotations are taken from the Holy Bible, New Living Translation, copyright ©1996, 2004, 2007 by Tyndale House Foundation. Used by permission of Tyndale House Publishers, Inc., Carol Stream, Illinois 60188. All rights reserved.

Scripture taken from the New King James Version®. Copyright © 1982 by Thomas Nelson, Inc. Used by permission. All rights reserved.

Scriptures taken from the Holy Bible, New International Version®, NIV®. Copyright © 1973, 1978, 1984, 2011 by Biblica, Inc.™ Used by permission of Zondervan. All rights reserved worldwide. www.zondervan.com. The "NIV" and "New International Version" are trademarks registered in the United States Patent and Trademark Office by Biblica, Inc.™

Special Sales: Most Lucid Books titles are available in special quantity discounts. Custom imprinting or excerpting can also be done to fit special needs. Contact Lucid Books at info@lucidbooks.net.

CONTENTS

Foreword 7
Acknowledgements 9
Introduction 11
The Encounter 13
1972 Renault 17
New Life 31
About Us 35
Looking Back 39
Fast-forward 41
Wrap Up 47
Daddy Devos 49
Addendum 273

FOREWORD

I'm sure there are many people that think they have the best dad in the world. I am definitely one of those people. My dad has been there through the most difficult times in my life. He's always believed in me, encouraged me, and has been a voice of godly wisdom and advice, pointing me to my true Heavenly Father in every circumstance.

This book contains several of these moments from my life as well as many more amazing encounters from my dad's. It is a true story that takes you on a journey that didn't necessarily begin with God, but after several audible encounters with Him, as well as some hysterical and unexpected moments, our family found itself forever changed. I hope that you will be encouraged and hear the Lord as you find yourself relating to different scenarios and people throughout the book.

Elisa Lin Haake

So... about my dad. He is one of the most genuine people you could ever meet. He knows what it means to practice what you preach. He spends more time on the former than the latter though, which I find admirable. So many people spend their whole lives preaching, but no practice is put in place to validate the words coming out of their mouths. My dad, John Michieli, is the real deal. The idea of "Daddy Devos" was birthed out of my father's love for our family and those around him, as well as the responsibility of being the spiritual covering for us in the midst of one of the lowest valleys in our history. Through these low points in our lives, there is nothing greater than knowing that your father is thinking of you and praying for your well being and God's blessing on your life every single day.

My Dad taught me that principles will always trump methods. I mention this because the principles found in this book, in whatever method they are applied, will have a wealth of return to the father, mother, or person who chooses to implement them in their own lives and families. People are not cookie cutters, so methods will not always work. However, principles will. This book and the principles in it have wisdom that will bring your family closer and will take you to new levels of trust in the Lord and His unending ability to provide and take care of you and your family.

Johnny Paris Michieli

ACKNOWLEDGEMENTS

I have written this manuscript over the past two years with the help and support of my family and friends. If it weren't for them, this work wouldn't have come to fruition. I am very grateful to the following special individuals who made this possible.

I would first, and most importantly, like to thank my wife Linda for thirty-four wonderful years of marriage. You have encouraged me when I was discouraged, loved me when I was unlovable, and most of all you are truly my best friend.

My thanks to Elisa Lin and Johnny Paris for being the absolute best kids a parent could have asked for, not to mention writing the greatest foreword ever.

A couple more individuals I would like to mention are the late Rick Wright (Uncle Rick) and Tammy Kleck. Rick literally spent hours going over punctuation and content with me prior to submitting this for publication. Tammy was the first person outside of our family to read it in its oh-so-rough form, and she gave me some very valuable input.

My love and thanks,
John

INTRODUCTION

In many ways, looking back over the past fifty-nine years gives me chills. I break out in goose bumps by just thinking about what has transpired. It has been an absolutely marvelous journey, much like the kind that is usually associated with Disney, Dreamworks, and Pixar.

I found myself alone one morning in Portland, sitting in my map-upholstered recliner, getting ready to begin my morning routine of reading the Bible. As I began to read, I became painfully aware that the house I was sitting in was quite empty. It was devoid of the things that had given it life in years gone by: my family, friends, laughter, and the aroma of something good simmering on the stove top. Yes, there I was all by myself. My wife and kids had moved to the Lone Star State of Texas some two thousand miles away, and I stayed behind to try to sell our depreciating piece of real estate in a rapidly declining market. As I turned away from what I was feeling and back to the Good Book, I felt a distinct impression. It wasn't an actual voice, just an impression. I knew the difference because I had heard God's audible voice on four previous occasions. The impression was that I should begin sending a daily scripture to my family. It would be a way to build them up (as well as me) and let them know that Dad, way up in the Pacific Northwest, was thinking of them. The only catch was how to send it to each family member at the same time.

There was this new thing, at least new to me, they called texting that seemed like a neat way to accomplish exactly what I wanted. So I approached my son, Johnny, and asked how it was done. As he began to explain it to me, it turned out to be a whole lot less complicated than I expected, and I came to find out "everyone" was doing it. This was fantastic. Little did I know how much it would impact me and my family from that point forward. Come with me; I'd like to take you on our journey.

THE ENCOUNTER

Over the past thirty-four years, Linda and I have had many opportunities to exercise and grow in our faith. It wasn't until we felt the Lord impress upon us to relocate from our home in Portland, Oregon, to Dallas, Texas, that we realized just how important that faith was. What happened over the next two years took us on a path that required courage and a big dose of faith. Time and time again the Lord reminded us of the landmarks and milestones, which confirmed that it was He who was directing our steps (...the steps of a good man are ordered of the Lord, Ps 37:23 NKJV). The book of James says that "when" we encounter various trials, we are to count it all "joy." Most people read that verse and usually insert the word "if" for the word "when," but that is not what James said, nor did he intend anything different. He knew from his own experience that "when" would best express what the Lord had wanted him to write. It has been (and continues to be) our experience that James' selection of words was right. Trials come! It all began fifty-four years ago when the Lord, in His infinite wisdom, chose to reveal Himself to a young, impressionable, small-town boy, in an almost fantasy-like way.

It was the custom in the Michieli household for those of us five years and under to take afternoon naps. On this particular day, for some reason unbeknownst to me, my sister was put down for her nap, but I was allowed to stay up. My sister and I were virtually inseparable back then, so this posed a very interesting and formidable challenge. What to do? Without my little sister, I had to make a decision, so I determined to venture out on my own. We lived on twenty acres growing up, much of which was open pasture while the rest had patches of trees - Locusts, Elms, and Russian Olives. As I proceeded to hike down to our regular play spot in the lower ten acres, something very peculiar happened.

I was coming out of what we used to call the Locust Forest, heading for the huge row of Elm trees at the northernmost edge of the property. Suddenly, out of nowhere, a blinding light flashed in the midst of a Russian Olive thicket and out walked a man. Now to a five-year-old who had been given a nap reprieve without anyone to play with, this was a most opportune event. Suddenly, I was no longer bereft of a playmate. Here was a rather unique looking man, with long dark hair, a beard, a white flowing robe, and sandals. He was the classic Sunday School Jesus, and he was walking toward me. It was absolutely perfect - I now had a playmate.

There was definitely something different about this guy. As he approached, two short tree stumps appeared out of nowhere, right next to me. I don't know how it would have impacted you, but to the five-year-old version of me, this guy was very cool. I watched Him carefully as he came towards me. He looked deeply into my eyes. It was as if He could see into my heart. Then he smiled and posed the question, "Would you like to sit down?" I had never experienced a look and smile like that before. Mind you, I was only five, but there was a feeling of peace that permeated my little body. Naturally I said, "OK." My recollection of how much time went by and the rest of our conversation remains hazy.

There are two things I remember clearly. First, I remember the tone of his voice—it was relaxing and comforting. Second, I remember the question he asked at the end of our conversation. "Do you know what you're here for?"

Without hesitation I replied, "Yes, I do." Even at that young age, I knew my life had a purpose that somehow would involve helping others. After I answered his question, we both stood, the stumps instantly disappeared, and my new-found friend walked back into the Russian Olive thicket. The Bible tells us that we are to be childlike in our faith. Well, I was five years old and what just happened was real - no question about it.

I tried to follow Him to the thicket, but He wasn't there. I ran back to where the stumps had been, but there was no trace..... He was gone! Excited, I ran for the house. Out of breath, bursting in the door, I found my mother sitting at one of those old fashioned 1950's ironing machines. I blurted out, "I talked to Jesus, I talked to Jesus, I talked to Jesus."

She casually responded, "No, you didn't," and returned to her ironing. Of course I was left speechless, knowing the experience I just had, and trying somehow in my little five-year-old mind to reconcile the words my mother uttered. I never spoke of the encounter again until the fall of my twenty-fourth year.

1972 RENAULT

After four years of college, studying such things as environmental studies, recreation administration, and secondary education without obtaining a degree, I became disillusioned with the whole school thing. I really didn't know what I wanted to do with my life. So I decided to travel the country and live out of the back of my pickup for the better part of the next couple of years. Bruce, one of my best friends from high school, accompanied me on what turned out to be an almost fourteen thousand mile escapade.

We began this quest from our home town of Hermiston, Oregon, and ended it in New Orleans, Louisiana. What happened in between? Let me give you some of the highlights. The early 1970's was a time when you could actually pull something like this off. As a parent today, I'd never agree to such a trip for any kid of mine. My parents were of a similar mindset back then, but I didn't exactly ask. I purchased a 1970 burnt orange Dodge pickup and put a canopy on the back. Bruce was a finish carpenter, so he transformed the back into a two-bed bungalow. Off we went down the western US coast. We didn't make many stops, but Big Sur and the Hearst Castle stand out as highlights. Upon reaching the LA area in southern California, we crashed at my aunt's house for the night. The next day, just before we departed, my aunt slipped me a little New Testament and said it might come in handy sometime. She also mentioned that she'd been praying for me. I had no idea the power of her prayers. After one night there, we were off for the west coast of Mexico and the Pacific beaches.

Our first glance of Mexico was Tijuana. After getting thoroughly lost right after crossing the border, we turned around, headed back to San Diego, and took Interstate 8 east to Tucson. We stayed a couple of days near the University of Arizona, we once again headed south, figuring a smaller port of entry, Nogales, would be less confusing to navigate. As it turned out, we were right. We spent our first night in Mexico on the Gulf of California in the little town of Guaymas. We met up with a group of college students and proceeded to paint the town. I'm still not sure exactly what color we painted it, but after patronizing every bar the town had to offer, the general consensus was that a good time was had by all. The next day we departed for more southern ports of call. Our destination of choice was Mazatlan, a good nine hundred miles away. The one thing about freelance travel is that you can do whatever you want whenever you want, and we both decided after driving all day that we wanted fresh seafood for dinner. Mazatlan was still some distance away. We took out our trusty map and found a road headed west, which ended at a little town on the Gulf of California called Topolobampo. It was a twenty-mile drive, ten of which was dirt road, and was still daylight on the way in. We found the ideal spot to have our seafood meal. This little restaurant was right on the wharf overlooking the marina, and kids were actually hand-carrying the fish from the boats to the restaurant. How much fresher does seafood get than that? As I was savoring every bite of my meal, Bruce asked if I was ok. Apparently my beet red face and sweating ears concerned him. I replied, "This is the best food I have ever tasted." Indeed it was not only the best, but the hottest, and it showed.

The next day we arrived in Mazatlan. The following two weeks flew by. We spent most of our daylight hours on the beach avoiding the street vendors, trying to blend in, and soaking in some color. I hooked up with some locals for a few pick-up basketball games at a nearby park. Our evenings and nights were filled with restaurants, bars, and nightlife. We were warned about drinking the water, so we purchased bottled water from the office of the RV Park where we were staying. It was much cheaper than buying it downtown;

however, the bargain was short lived when I walked into the office and saw them filling our five-gallon jug from the tap. We concluded that cervezas were probably more compatible to our health. Fortunately, neither of us was any worse for wear, and we ended up leaving town not long after that.

We soon realized that our three years of grammatical Spanish in high school allotted us enough speaking skills to get into trouble, but unfortunately, not enough to get out. Our next official stop was Guadalajara. Some people had told us there was a huge market there worth exploring, and they were right. We spent the day wandering from shop to shop, purchasing some souvenirs and partaking in the local sport of bartering. That night we went to a nightclub and ended up having to bribe our way out. Here is what happened. We discovered the drinks the girls sitting with us were pounding down (drinks we were generously paying for) were just colored water. Bruce started to make a scene because we had obviously been set up. There was a brief altercation with a bouncer, and before he could call the authorities, I had my wallet out. $100 later, we vacated the premises unscathed. This is where it might have been helpful to have a better handle of the language.

The next week and a half were spent mostly behind the wheel. We stopped at a few of the historical sights, one of which was the Museum of Natural History in Mexico City. We saw the Mayan pyramids near Veracruz (where we learned how to eat sugar cane), Veracruz harbor, the fruit orchards of the eastern Mexican coast (the tangerines were to die for), and we enjoyed a little Mescal on the beach near Tampico. From there we continued north for the US border.

We entered the good ole USA at Brownsville, Texas, and beelined it for a McDonald's. Ahhhh, we ordered in English and sunk our teeth into an American hamburger. I remember thinking, "It doesn't get any better than this." I think my taste has changed because I can't even contrive that sort of feeling for a McDonald's burger now. Anyway, after some discussion and a look at our finances, Bruce and I decided to head for New Orleans. It was about as far as we thought we could get and have enough money left over for a place to live while we were looking for work. It took about three weeks before we were both gainfully employed. We had a lot of fun for about six months, then we got restless and wanted to travel again. Off we went. It was the spring of 1975, and sixteen states later, we landed back in our favorite spot, New Orleans. We didn't find it as easy to get jobs this time, and unbeknownst to me the direction of my life was about to change.

The place was Loyola Avenue in New Orleans near City Hall where the Superdome was being constructed. Bruce and I were driving home from work in my pick-up when I heard a voice out of nowhere say aloud, "You have places to go, people to meet and they aren't here in New Orleans. You need to go home."

I looked over at Bruce and asked, "What did you say?"

He answered, "I didn't say anything."

About that time, I lost a hubcap, so I turned the truck around in order to retrieve it. As we approached the spot where the hubcap fell off, I heard the same voice again, "You have places to go, people to meet and they aren't here in New Orleans. You need to go home."

I turned to Bruce again. "What did you say?"

He gave the same reply, "I didn't say anything." He gave me a weird look and I kept driving.

Something was happening inside of me..... I was blanketed with an overwhelming peace. I knew that it was time to end our journey and move on with my life. I turned to Bruce and said, "I don't know how, when, where, or why, but I have places to go, people to meet and they aren't here in New Orleans - I have to go home." He wasn't ready to go but was fine with me leaving.

I was out of cash and had no funds to get there, but the "peace" outweighed all of that. Once we arrived at our small uptown apartment, I began exploring all the possibilities which would get my travel-weary body back home to Oregon.

It was mid-December 1975, and my search didn't last long. Bruce and I had a few ideas, but they ultimately ended with a collect call to my parents in Hermiston. After explaining my situation, most of it involving my perception of how destitute I was, the words sort of flowed from my lips. "How would you like to buy me a one way ticket home for Christmas this year?" Their answer was affirmative. They weren't thrilled about me taking this trip in the first place, so when the opportunity to end it presented itself, they were relieved and more than happy to oblige. I had already planned to leave my pickup with Bruce. That evening, I showed up at the Western Union office to collect my Christmas gift - $175 cash. I packed my few belongings, and within twenty-four hours of hearing that compelling audible voice on Loyola Avenue, I was on a plane bound for the great Pacific Northwest. I remember it feeling almost surreal as I stepped off that little twin engine plane in Pendleton, thirty minutes from my hometown. I was thinking about where I had been the past couple years, uncertain as to what lay ahead. It was that voice I heard in the pickup and the sense of peace that called me home. That voice - it somehow was so familiar. I knew I'd heard it before, but couldn't, for the life of me, recall when or where. I didn't realize it at the time, but later connected the dots, that the voice was identical to the man I met in the Locust Forest many years before. Now I was back home and thankful for parents who cared for not only me, but all of my siblings. They supported us in spite of our oh-so-obvious weaknesses. As I look back now, I relate that caring to the same way the Lord looks at us. No matter what mistakes we make or circumstances we find ourselves in, He forgives and accepts us and takes us in. So I moved in with my parents, confident that I would be able to find a job right away and be on my own shortly.

Well, my job hunting experience turned into a drawn out affair during which my little sister offered to let me share the house she was renting. Finally, four months into my search, I landed a job with a surveying firm. The very same week I received my first paycheck, I also received thirteen weeks of unemployment checks totaling about $700. My claim had been under dispute since my return to Oregon in December. I endorsed them right away and presented them to my folks for their awesome generosity. What occured over the next several months was like a dream and resulted in an experience I can only describe as divinely orchestrated into the front seat of a 1972 Renault.

Since I hadn't been part of the social scene in my home town for a while, it was high time to get reacquainted. Another friend of mine from high school, Dan, encouraged me to join a local slow-pitch softball team sponsored by Smitty's Pancake House. The little smiley pancakes on our backs struck fear in the hearts of our opponents. We were definitely a team to be reckoned with. We won a lot of games but usually fell a little short when it came to winning the big one. With work, practice, games, and tournaments, I had limited time to enjoy my other interests like swimming, tennis, golf, girls, etc. As spring turned into summer, Dan and I found ourselves in our team restaurant, Smitty's, where the team members got some sort of discount. We were wearing our bright orange uniforms and grabbing a quick bite before our game. Our waitress, a gal neither of us recognized, came up to our table, and with a very enthusiastic, bubbly greeting said, "May I take your order?" We gave her our order, and as she walked away Dan said, "I'll flip you for her!" She was obviously new in town, and of course, one of us had to be hospitable and ask her out.

I replied, "OK."

He came back with, "Heads I lose; tails you win." After we conducted the coin flip as a formality, Dan looked at me and said, "She's too nice for me, you take her out." He always did have a sense of humor, and she was nice!

There was something about this girl that was different than the other girls around town. We finished our dinner, and as we took care of the check, she jokingly said that she was the "new girl" in town.... I don't exactly remember the rest. I didn't waste any time. I asked her what time she got off. "Later", she said.

"No problem. I'll be home after our game. Why don't you stop by when you get off?" Well, I didn't expect to see her again until my next visit to Smitty's, but what the heck, it was worth a shot. Dan and I took off to our game and upon returning home, I had forgotten our little exchange at Smitty's. After jumping in the shower, I decided to catch up with the characters in a interesting book I had been reading. No sooner had I started when I heard a knock at the door, and that little conversation we had while paying the check instantly came back. There she was the new girl in town, standing at my front door. I was a little surprised, but didn't want to show it. I'm sure I acted as if I had been expecting her. We sat and talked for a couple of hours, having a great time. Then she looked at the clock and told me she really needed to go as it was getting late. I asked when her next day off was, and we set an official date. As she drove away into the night, I stood in kind of a daze and couldn't help but wonder what just happened? Linda Brown, that's what!

When I left New Orleans several months earlier, I entrusted my only means of transportation to my buddy Bruce. I told him that once I got established, I'd let him know, and he could drive the truck back to Oregon. At the time I reassured him that if he really wanted to return to Louisiana, I would buy a one way ticket for him and pay for the gas it took to get the truck to Oregon. Sure enough, in April of 1976, Bruce pulled up in front of the house we were renting. It was great to see him and spend a couple days catching up. Then, transaction complete, he headed off into the wild blue yonder, back to New Orleans.

Over the next few months that first meeting with Linda Brown led to an almost daily rendezvous. One evening while Linda was with me, my phone rang and without thinking it through, I planned a date with one of my other girlfriends. Note to self: dumb move. You can probably guess what happened next. I don't remember her exact words, but, I believe the conversation went something like this.

Linda: Who was that?
Me: So and so. (I gave Linda her name)
Linda: Did you just do what I think you did?

Me: Well, she invited me to a grand opening party on Thursday.
Linda: I don't think this is going to work. I'm a one-man woman, and it appears you're not a one-woman man.
Me: What do you mean by that? (having just one girlfriend at a time was a whole new line of thinking for me.)
Linda: I mean you're going to have to make a decision here. It's either me or her.
Me: (That one took me off guard, and I had to think for a minute. It probably felt like an eternity to Linda.) I choose you!
Linda: (Appearing a little more relaxed) So are you going ahead with your date Thursday?
Me: Yes, but I'll tell her of my decision. (I did by the way, much to the other girl's dismay.)

At that point, Linda and I were officially a number. Hardly a day passed by that we didn't see or call each other. August was there before we knew it, and she had to return to Portland Bible College for her second year. During those two summer months, Linda and I grew so close we were almost inseparable. In fact, the night before she was to leave, I went over to her apartment and was helping her get her things together and somehow, in the middle of folding towels and packing her suitcases, I looked up with tears in my eyes and said something I had been very cautious about, not having ever uttered the words before. 'Linda, I love you.'

Hearing those words from me for the very first time brought on a conflicting set of emotions for her. On the one hand, she admitted, "I love you too." On the other hand, her internal conflict was based on being a Christian, and that brought on a whole onslaught of thoughts and feelings she hadn't had to face directly until those words entered the atmosphere. She was instantly torn, knowing in her heart that dating a non-Christian guy (keep in mind that although I was a nice, respectful, good, and handsome guy, I was clearly not a Christian) should have been absolutely out of the question for her, and falling in love unthinkable. From the very first night she appeared on my doorstep, she had gone against everything she believed in. Looking across the room, she could tell I was speaking the truth, and she felt the exact same way. "We fell in love. This can't be happening," she thought. She never saw it coming. So with all the moral fiber she could muster, and in one big breath, she made this statement. "You know, when I leave tomorrow, we'll probably never see each other again."

Totally ignoring her comment, I replied with, "Why don't you come by the house tomorrow on your way out of town, so I can say good bye." We hugged, she finished packing, and I went home.

The next day proved to be very eventful in quite an unusual way. Linda arrived at my place sometime midmorning with the resolve that she would most likely never see me again. I came out to her car, a 1972 Renault, and as always invited her in. She respectfully declined and said she had to get going. We talked a little and said our good-byes. She reiterated what she had said earlier - that we would most likely never see each other again, to which I responded, again ignoring her comment, "Call me collect when you get there." She rolled up her window and began driving west down Juniper Avenue.

As I watched her car progress down the street, it happened again! The very same voice I heard in New Orleans, the same voice from the Locust Forest. This time that voice came audibly, loud and clear in my ear. I heard, "You're going to marry that girl." I wheeled around, looking to see if anyone was there, but there wasn't. As I turned toward the house, I was enveloped in the same warmth and "peace" I had felt as a five-year-old. I was going to marry that girl! I knew in my knower, and that settled it. As I entered the front door, my sister was sitting in the living room, and the first words out of my mouth were, "There goes the girl I'm going to marry."

She looked at me and said, "No way, I'd never put you two together." I walked away smiling. About 5:30 that evening the phone rang and guess what? It was a collect call from you-know-who.

Shortly thereafter, my oldest brother Bruce invited me to live with him in Eugene, Oregon. I gave notice to my employer, packed up my earthly belongings, and moved to the home of the fighting Ducks, where I had previously attended college. I got a job and began commuting back and forth to Portland on the weekends to see, who else, Linda Brown.

In late October, Linda's conflict of emotions surfaced again. Our relationship so far had been under the radar, and only her closest friends even knew who I was. She felt uncomfortable/convicted and finally came to a place of surrender to her core beliefs. She made her final decision.

Her conviction was in the Biblical truth of not being unequally yoked with an unbeliever, me (2 Corinthians 6:14). Not to mention the fact that dating an unbeliever can open a whole can of worms, not very many of which actually catch fish. With me a twist was thrown in. She had unintentionally fallen in love with me. She was just playing around and it turned into love. That being said, there was no denying the depth of conviction she was feeling from the Lord.

Looking back, I can now totally understand where she was coming from. When a believer dates an unbeliever and shares the Lord with him or her, more often than not, the unbelieving person, especially if they really like/love the believer, may try to fabricate an experience with the Lord. But the reality is that many times they will manufacture an experience in order to convince themselves and the believer. The genuineness of such an experience is almost always in question. In our case, we had a much different and very interesting outcome.

It was the last weekend in October of 1976, and as was normal for me on Friday nights after work, I hit I-5 north looking forward to seeing my Sweetie. Portland was about a two hour drive. I arrived at my aunt's apartment in Milwaukie, a suburb of Portland, in the late evening. My family was preparing to go out to eat and listen to Peter, Paul and Mary. This is not who you boomers may be thinking of, but rather two local brothers and their sister who were quite good. I had just told them that I would wait at the apartment until Linda arrived and catch up to them later, when in walked Linda with a very determined look. Now discernment wasn't my strong suit, but everyone else seemed to pick up on it and quickly dismissed themselves leaving us to discuss whatever that determined look was implying.

Linda had just come from a Friday night praise and worship meeting at a church called New Song. She had been wrestling with something she felt she needed to say to me all week and felt like God gave her the courage to follow through that night. I soon discovered what was behind that look she had displayed when she arrived. We engaged in some very awkward small talk, and shortly into it she could no longer continue. She had to tell me what was on her heart. Back when we first started seeing each other, Linda casually had told me she had a "friend" that "loved" me, which had been the extent of her mentioning the Lord the whole time we had known each other. I later found out that was most unusual for her. She normally expressed her faith openly. Well, it was at this point that she chose to bring up her "friend" again. She began to go through how the Lord had been dealing with her. How her relationship to the Lord and being a Christian was the most important thing in her life. Our dating was totally contrary to everything she believed in, and because of those beliefs, we had to break up. I was shocked. We talked about it, but there was no detouring her. With tears dripping down my face, I pulled myself together and asked if she would consider staying awhile even though we "broke up." After all, I drove up just to see her, and by now she was my best friend. Linda's reply was very matter of fact and to the point. She said she had mid-terms coming up, so if I wanted to help her study for her exams, she would stay. I agreed so she took out her books along with some study questions.

As it so happens, the particular test she was studying for was the Tabernacle of Moses. I knew absolutely nothing about the Bible other than it seemed to me to be a book people who go to church generally have around but do not open. Not being a church going guy, it was completely foreign to me. She handed me some of the questions, and with that, the night began. I became more and more curious with each question and listened intently to her answers. I had always had a somewhat undeveloped interest in history, so in between her questions, I began inserting some of my own. After she would recite an answer, I would come back with, "Why did they do that? And for what purpose?" We went back and forth for hours going over the various details of sacrifice preparation, the altar, washing at the laver, entering the Holy Place, the preparing of the bread, the burning of incense, trimming the wicks on the candlestick, checking the oil, the veil, all leading to the ultimate and triumphal entry into the Holy of Holies, the Mercy Seat, and into the very presence of God Himself. Even though the hurt of her breaking up with me was still there, this material was fascinating and captured all my attention. We totally lost sight of the time, and it was well past midnight. Linda started to get ready to go, but because of the lateness of the hour, I asked her if she wanted to sleep on the couch. She reluctantly agreed.

Morning came, and Portland was greeted by a typical gray, dreary, overcast fall day. It was literally pouring rain. Even getting from the front door to the car without getting soaked was a challenge. I followed her to her car and leaned on the driver's side window, trying to talk to her amidst the downpour. We both realized this wasn't going to work, so she invited me inside the car. We really didn't say much - mostly because we planned not to see each other again. Then, out of nowhere, Linda doubled her fist, hit the steering wheel, and said, "I don't understand why people won't accept something that is free." I had no idea what she was talking about, and as I looked across the console at her, she asked, "Remember when I said I had a "Friend" that loves you?"

I answered, "Yes."

As she stared at the steering wheel, never once looking up, she came back with, "Would you like to meet Him?" You have to understand something here. Linda held a very strong conviction regarding what was referred to as "Missionary

Dating" - the concept of dating a non-Christian with the hope of bringing them to the Lord. This is the reason she never said much to me about God. This form of dating was frowned on by the church because it almost always ended in a relational disaster. The girl leads the guy to the Lord, the guy goes through the motions but never really gets saved, they go on to get married, and a host of problems ensue. Needless to say, this was Linda's biggest fear, and here she was right on the precipice of that possibility. She couldn't believe the words that had just crossed her lips. She explained all this to me later.

The event that followed was expected yet in some ways a surprise. It was supernatural and ended in the miraculous. She found herself asking me the very question she had, up until that day, avoided. "Would you like to meet Him?" My answer was, "Yes." In my mind, I was thinking there must be some sort of prayer that was to follow. Linda hesitated as a million thoughts flooded her mind in a split second, which I've learned since is a normal occurence for women. She now felt obligated to lead this guy to the Lord. At the same time she had just put herself in a position she never ever wanted to be in. Resigning herself to the fact that she was already there, the next step had to be taken.

With her thoughts racing like a high speed internet connection, and with me waiting in the wings for a reply, she said to herself, "Ok Lord, I've already messed up. You're going to have to do this-it has to be You so John knows it is real." Then Linda, never once looking in my direction, said in a very deliberate voice, "I'll pray, then you pray." She closed her eyes tight and started. I didn't have a clue, but I thought, "She knows what she's doing," so I remained silent. She began with, "Thank you, Lord, for this beautiful day. Here's John."

I looked over and said, "What do I say?"

Never once opening her eyes, she replied, "You know what to say!" As I turned back to what I considered a prayer posture, eyes closed, head bowed, I just let go. I could hardly believe what began to come out of my mouth.

It started with, "Lord, please forgive me for what I have done and for not doing the things I should have done." Then I began to pray through the Tabernacle of Moses, beginning at the brazen altar, understanding I deserved judgment, offering myself as a sacrifice; continuing to the laver, asking God to wash and cleanse me; followed by entering the Holy Place, asking Him to accept the incense of my prayer; and finally walking into the very presence of God - into the Holy of Holies. I began to weep uncontrollably and remember repeating, "Thank you Jesus, thank you Jesus, thank you Jesus," over and over again. In that instant, there was a miracle, a transformation which took place. My spirit was rejuvenated, regenerated, and reborn. It was absolutely exhilarating. It felt as if a huge weight, which I didn't even realize I had, was lifted off my shoulders. As I looked up from my prayer, there was Linda, wide-eyed, staring at me in a state of shock. She could hardly believe what she had just witnessed, but knew without a doubt that God had shown up, taken her desperate prayer, and the miraculous happened - John got saved! No doubt about it. She had come in obedience and humility with total separation in mind and executed the plan to perfection. But in His ultimate wisdom, God, with His unconditional love, at the last second, seized the moment and breathed life into what she considered to be dead. He presented her with a brand spankin' new, Christian boyfriend all in a 1972 Renault.

A NEW LIFE

As I exited the Renault, Linda and I said our good-byes. This time we had an unspoken sense that our once finished relationship had somehow started anew. Neither of us had anticipated this. I literally floated back to my aunt's apartment. I don't recall my feet touching the ground. I think I even had to duck to get through the door. I had just fallen in love all over again, but this time it was with my long lost friend. My friend from the Locust Forest. Now He was my Lord and Savior, Jesus Christ. This brief and meaningful encounter with the Lord Himself changed the direction of my entire life. October 29, 1976, was indelibly written on my heart.

What took place during the month and a half following was again nothing short of miraculous. I went to a place I had only been once in the past 19 years - church. The last memory I had of church was "you could hear a pin drop silence." It was boring. In Sunday School we made paper chains, listened to Bible stories, and then were quizzed. It seemed like the right answer was always - Jesus. That was the extent of my church involvement, so naturally a part of me was a little apprehensive. Linda took me to a Sunday evening service at her church in Portland, at that time it was called Bible Temple. It had absolutely no resemblance to my previous church experience. There was contemporary music and singing. People were friendly, upbeat, lifting their hands, and even dancing. I loved it! If this was church, bring it on!! I met a lot of folks who obviously really knew the Lord personally. The one person that made the biggest impact on me was Pastor Dick Iverson. Linda scheduled a time for us to share our story with him. When we shook hands, he looked into my eyes, and I instantly knew that look. A flood of emotions and memories came streaming into my heart. In a flash my thoughts transported me back to when I was five-years-old, and my encounter with Jesus. The look in Pastor Iverson's eyes reflected the same peace, acceptance, and warmth I had felt in the Locust Forest so many years ago.

Within weeks, not only did my view of church change, but I began to change. I found myself showing up as often as the doors were open. I was baptized in water, filled with the Holy Spirit, and I devoured the Bible. Linda had flippantly told me after I got saved that I couldn't be a Christian if I didn't read the Bible every day. I took it literally and committed to read it when I got up, at my lunch breaks, and before I went to bed. I even slept with it under my pillow, hoping I would somehow absorb it while I was sleeping. I read it from cover to cover three times my first year, and after thirty-five years, I still love and read it on a daily basis. Back in the '80s I heard someone say the B.I.B.L.E. is our Basic Instructions Before Leaving Earth. It's the manual, so I read it..... In fact, my reading is one of the major reasons for this book. I realize that you don't have to read the Bible everyday to be a Christian, but that was actually the best piece of advice I ever received.

My relationship with Linda began to blossom, even though I was still living in Eugene. I could hardly get through the week in anticipation of seeing her and getting to go to church and feel the presence of God - twice every Sunday. I wrote to her weekly, sometimes daily, aside from the fact that we talked almost every day. By the way, Linda still has the majority, if not all, of those love letters filled with "Sweet Everythings" as we affectionately referred to them. You have to remember that all we had thirty years ago were land lines with long distance charges and snail mail.

My brother Bruce really didn't know what to think as this transformation began to unfold in my life. He observed me reading the Bible at every spare moment. As I pressed deeper and deeper into the Word, insights would come, and along with the insights, questions would arise. Being new to this Christian lifestyle, I became like an enormous sponge, soaking in teaching but mostly devouring the Word. I had the privilege of sitting under some of the most profound teachers and Biblical scholars of our day. My spiritual foundation was being shaped. It was like living in a bubble with impenetrable walls. I felt God's blessing in so many ways. I began to get scriptures to share with Linda on a daily basis. I've found that when I'm in the Word, God has an open conduit through which to speak into my life. I was definitely trying to open the valve as wide as possible.

In Deuteronomy 28, we find one of the smallest words with the biggest reward in the Bible, "if". If we will obey His commands, then He will bless our going out, coming in, the work we do, and the time we rest! This encompassed every area of my life. That season of my life was truly awesome! I give the leadership of Bible Temple a lot of credit in those early days. Being connected to a Bible College, they were committed to being a "teaching church." Foundations were an integral part of the curriculum, and the focus was on the raising up of leaders. All in all it was a very powerful way to be launched into a new life. I could not have dreamed up a better scenario to begin a new spiritual walk with God. My previous life, in terms of goals and purpose, had all but disappeared, and my future lay before me. Somehow the Lord knew what I needed (imagine that) and set my feet firmly on that path.

ABOUT US

The path Linda and I were on was becoming increasingly obvious. The anticipation of my arrival in Portland each weekend became the highlight of our week. I turned my pen into a woven network of letters, sometimes as many as three to four per week. They were filled with intrigue, drama, laughter, fun, disguise, and love. Expectation was the stage, she and I the main players, with a myriad of cameo appearances. One particular episode comes to mind in which I wrote several pages describing the process by which I was going incognito. In good fun, I was verbose, but illusive. By the end of the week, the suspense was just about killing her. As it turned out, I was simply growing a mustache, but the intrigue of it all was keeping her on pins and needles. She was actually a little concerned about the transformation I was alluding to. My entrance was anticlimactic when she realized this was all about a mustache. With letters in hand, she exclaimed, "All this for that?" It was all great fun. The mustache, by the way, is still with me today and remains the only thing which would prompt the "D" word - jokingly, of course. I have shaved it a few times only to be encouraged to fertilize my upper lip within a few hours of doing so. A decade or so before this writing, I added the goatee I now sport. The fashion reviews have been so positive, I have to keep it.

It was sometime during the winter months after reading Genesis 22 for the third time that I felt God prompting me to give Linda up - I mean break up with her - with the full intention of ending our relationship. It was the part in chapter 22 where Abraham is asked by God to take Isaac up the mountain and present him as a sacrifice, only to have God stop him as he was raising his hand to go through with it. I remember so vividly the impression that came over me. I asked myself, "Am I serving the Lord because I want to be with Linda?" After all, it was her greatest fear in leading me to the Lord in the first place. "Or am I serving the Lord because I have my own genuine and intimate relationship with Him?" As I wrestled between those diametrically opposed thoughts, I knew in my heart that I had to have a clarity on this.

The first question that popped into my head was this: "Do you love Me enough to lay your relationship with Linda on the altar as Abraham did with his only son Isaac - totally allowing it to die with the full realization that it might never be resurrected again?"

Here I was, a new Christian being confronted with an extremely difficult decision. The big question for me was what was my motive for serving Him? I wanted to know.... I called Linda and told her what was going on—how I felt like the Lord was really dealing with me, and that I wouldn't be coming to Portland that weekend. The rub was that I also had to break up with her. This was excruciatingly difficult, but we both knew the uncertainty had to be cleared up and this was the only way. After we hung up, I immediately fell on my face before the Lord. I told Him I had to know if this was MY relationship that had been kindled over the past several months, or if I was simply going through the motions so that I could maintain the attachment which had grown so strong between Linda and me. I read and reread that passage in Genesis 22, so aware that I had just let go of the love of my life. My mind went back to the previous summer, and I reminded the Lord of what He had spoken to me so directly. "There goes the girl you're going to marry."

"What about that?" I asked Him. The Lord and I went back and forth for the better part of three hours that evening. Finally, after feeling like Jacob wrestling with God, I felt a breakthrough and the conclusion was that, with or without Linda, I was going to serve the Lord. This truly was MY personal relationship with Him, not some vicarious thing I was doing to get a prize. Once again, I opened the Word and began to read Genesis 22. This time I was enveloped with a sense of God's love, a God who was willing to sacrifice His only Son for me, John Michieli, so that I might live and have a very close and ongoing friendship with that very same Son. In that moment, the peace that I experienced was a Phillippians 4 kind of peace that passes all understanding. The release had come. Now I could call Linda and share it with her. I knew that it was settled, and He had given Linda back to me.

What I learned through those difficult hours was that God was as committed to giving me the answer as I was to pursue it. So I picked up the phone, called her, filled her in on all that had happened and told her I would be on my way to Portland the next day after all. Needless to say, Linda was thrilled!

In the months following we discussed future ministry, children, family—virtually everything. Before making any plans, I had a couple of hurdles to overcome. The first was her dad, who turned out to be pretty easy. He told me with a smile, "If you can handle her, you can have her - just don't bring her back." You have to know Linda's dad to appreciate his humor. The second one, her Aunt Jackie, was of more "spiritual" importance to Linda because she and her Uncle Herb had been instrumental in Linda coming to know the Lord. Linda was very close to her Aunt Jackie, in some ways as close to her as she was to her own mother. She had a great relationship with her parents, they just weren't saved at the time. That being said, her Aunt Jackie had a way of imparting practical and spiritual wisdom to Linda. Linda knew Aunt Jackie loved her and could always depend on her to be honest with her. As we approached our first Thanksgiving holiday, Linda reminded me that the one person's approval we still needed was her Aunt Jackie's. Since I had not met her before, I was a little uneasy going into the holiday. However, once there, I found the whole family to be welcoming. Aunt Jackie was exactly as described, and she was delighted for Linda and I. Relieved, we began to make plans and continued on the path toward wedded bliss.

We spent Christmas with my family, who always seemed to like whoever I brought home, and Linda was no exception. My sister kind of thought Linda was too nice for me, which I took as a compliment.

When 1977 rolled around, I was still in Eugene. I joined an intramural church basketball league in Portland for the winter, followed by slow pitch softball in the spring and summer. It was a great way to meet new folks, not to mention the fact that sport brings out the true character in all of us. You really get to know what kind of "characters" you are playing with. As April showers turned to May flowers, Linda and I got engaged. Don't ask me how I proposed. Although I considered myself a modern day Romeo, I'll have to be honest and say I'm not so sure I actually did ask (more on that later). I recall buying rings, but the actual "proposal" is a bit blurry. We were excited and wanted a short engagement, so we approached Pastor Iverson to see if he would marry us and to check the church calendar. He responded, "I'd love to. How about August 20th?" He went on to say, "I already have about twenty couples ahead of you this summer." Love was in the air. I believe we were the twenty-fourth wedding that summer at Bible Temple.

I began plans to eliminate the commute. As we were now engaged, and with summer quickly approaching, I figured there was no better time to close the geographical gap. I turned down the promotion I was offered and gave my two-week notice instead, much to everyone's surprise. Wedding preparations now were in full swing. On August 20, 1977, our wedding day, at about 2:20 pm, as we knelt down to be prayed over, I leaned over to Linda and said, "Oh, by the way, will you marry me?" We still look back and chuckle at that moment to this day. Luckily, she said, "Yes!"

LOOKING BACK

Time flies when you are having fun, right? Well, as I look back on our 34-plus years together, I'm so grateful. Having attended four high school reunions, I realize what we have is a rarity. There are only a handful of us in the illustrious Hermiston High Class of 1970 who actually got married and managed to maintain that state for the duration. I say all that to get to this - Linda and I have something special - an added ingredient that has allowed us to grow together when many around us seemed to grow apart. When we took our vows to love, honor, and cherish one another, in sickness (this one really took its toll on us, by the way) and in health until death do us part, we meant it! I sometimes imagine what it would be like if the general populace would seriously take to heart the traditional vows that 95% of the weddings out there use. There would be a lot more happy marriages for sure. By the way, the added ingredient I mentioned a few sentences ago was not our vows. It was and is the One who created the sacred institution of marriage in the first place—God. We began our marriage as a tri-union. It kind of puts a new meaning to being a third wheel because without this third wheel, the union loses its strength and balance. Have you ever tried to ride a tricycle with a missing wheel? I think you get my point.

We got off to a very healthy start and attribute that to being surrounded by healthy examples of married couples in our church. There were classes and seminars, but, more importantly, there were living examples of "real", respectful, and loving couples. I guess you could say it rubbed off on us. I was trying to remember just how many weddings there were that eventful summer of '77. As I recall, it was around 26. I don't have any statistics on how many of those flourished through the years, but the couples we have kept in touch with, if asked, would probably attribute their success to the foundational teaching we all received. The teaching alone wouldn't have been successful had it not been for the examples we had all around us. We found out that who you spend time with can shape who you become.

We, like any honest couple, have had our challenges. Those who are close to us know that Linda and I have totally different personalities, strengths, and weaknesses. Some of the hurdles we have overcome could have taken us out, but "Thank God" we were both more committed to the Lord than each other. He gave us counsel that brought hope, healing, and a future. Together, iron has sharpened iron, and we love each other more today than anytime in the past.

As I said, from the day Linda and I said "I do", we not only were committed to each other, but also to serve the body of Christ. We wanted nothing more than to follow the Lord and do His will. As He began to stir our hearts, we entered into some of the most turbulent but also fulfilling times we have ever encountered. We have seen chapter after chapter open and close, each one deepening our belief that God really has a plan for our lives. Out of the many years of mountain tops and valleys have come these pages, which I hope will be an inspiration to all who take the time to not only read them but also put them to good use in cultivating the most precious institution in our society today - "the Family."

FAST-FORWARD

The idea of writing my story began while I was alone in Portland. However, it wasn't until our move to Texas that the inspiration for this work began to come together. It all started about four years ago. An associate of Linda's introduced her to a Texas based business opportunity. After some prudent research, we both felt it could turn into something very lucrative. The business appeared to be a good fit with what Linda was currently doing, and she could work from our home in Oregon or wherever. Having been born and raised as native Oregonians in the Beaver State, neither of us had ever dreamed of living anywhere outside the great Pacific Northwest. She had some initial limited success but was encouraged to visit Texas for a few weeks to really jump start her business. Well, after a couple of weeks down south, she realized the enormous potential and ended up extending her stay by several weeks. By the time she returned to Oregon, her new business endeavor had really taken off. We had intermittently prayed together about the business, but once it began to get some real traction, we were forced to see the obvious: if we were to live in Texas, the type of business we had would grow naturally. We could continue doing it from Oregon, but being out of state had its own set of challenges. So I set aside some serious time to pray. I was on a company trip to Alaska when I felt a strong impression that we should move to Texas. I picked up the phone, called Linda, and boldly announced to her and my daughter Elisa (by speaker phone) that I had been praying and we were moving to Texas. They were both somewhat surprised because, frankly, it was a little out of character for me to just announce something like this. At the same time, Linda in particular had grown to trust my "impressions". When I got my answer, I just knew.

The first phase of our move involved our daughter, Elisa. My wife's friend and business associate had offered to let her live with them and work for her until Elisa got established. That was a very generous offer, so we packed everything of Elisa's that we could fit into her little Dodge Neon, and off the three of us went for Texas. We arrived none the worse for wear. After a couple of days, I returned to Portland while Linda remained in Texas for a few more weeks helping Elisa make the transition while using her free time to build her business. We put our house in Portland on the market a few weeks before that first 2000 mile jaunt. The hope was that it would sell by year's end and that the three of us could find a place to settle in the Dallas area. We never anticipated what would unfold next.

Within a couple of weeks, we got an offer on our home. Our realtor felt it was solid, so we began discussing building plans with a contractor in Texas. Linda's business was progressing, and Elisa was settling in, or so we thought. Her situation was a bit different than most employer/employee relationships. Living where you work can prove to be a bit awkward at times since where you sleep is just down the hall from your desk. Plus, knowing the family from a distance can be very different from living and working with them every day. You probably already know where this is going. Elisa had communicated with us that her situation was getting uncomfortable several weeks into it, and she expressed interest in possibly looking for other full-time work. She was also working part-time at a restaurant when a position at Gateway Church had come up that she was very interested in. It was at this point that things took a turn for the worse.

One Sunday in mid-November 2007, we got a call from the family Elisa was staying with. There had been a gross misunderstanding, which resulted in Elisa having to leave their home with absolutely no notice. It goes without saying that this was a tremendous shock! Waves of emotion flooded us as we were very concerned about her. Where would she go? All we could do was sit helplessly by in Portland, Oregon, 2000 miles away. Fortunately, she managed to connect with a young lady who was generous enough to take her in. Thank You, Lord!

This was the start of something quite remarkable. Elisa applied and got the position at the church and received many accolades, including a promotion. These circumstances expedited our exodus. We agreed that temporarily Linda and Elisa should find an apartment and stay there until I could join them and move into the new home we were building. We flew Elisa in and back out for the holidays. The day after Christmas, Linda and I set about renting a small U-haul, filled it with the bare necessities needed for the apartment, and made our way back to Dallas again.

The previously described events happened over a six month period. When I returned, my company told me there were two different positions available that would have allowed me to transfer to Texas. However, after numerous delays, a hiring freeze was instituted in late 2007. It virtually eliminated my job offers. With company sales declining and department budgets being cut, it proved to be a most difficult time in which to relocate, both internally and externally. We were on the proverbial roller coaster ride - one minute thinking we were on the verge of breakthrough, only to have our hopes of reuniting as a family anytime soon dashed. Over the next 18 months, I rattled around in our nearly empty house. By the way, the offer on the house fell through. I oversaw a territory so my job still kept me in the Northwest, and it was lonely at best...my dog even died. I had a small reprieve, though, when my son moved home for a few months after graduating from college, giving me some welcomed company. It was during that time that the inspiration for Daddy Devotions began. I started each day by sending the family a scripture by text. After a few weeks of receiving them every day, the kids affectionately called them Daddy Devos. The one constant through the whole transition was my "Dd Today" texts. Living apart certainly can motivate you to action on things that otherwise might remain dormant.

In this case, it precipitated a daily family communiqué, which was originally designed as a tool to keep our immediate family encouraged. However, it soon expanded outside of our little circle to several of our kids' friends, not to mention a couple of our longtime family friends and colleagues. Once into it for a few months, Johnny approached me with the idea of putting these daily devotions into book form. When I started texting, the thought of writing a book was the furthest thing from my mind; however, after accumulating over 250 Daddy Devo's, as well as the positive feedback from the recipients, I began to warm-up to the concept.

Linda and Elisa were living in a small apartment in Bedford, Texas, while Johnny and I were staying in our house in Portland. It was only a few months after Linda had moved that Johnny got the itch to move as well. He had been happily employed at AT&T in Portland at the time, so he put in for a transfer and moved in March of 2008.

So there we were; Linda, Elisa, and now Johnny were living in Texas, and I was still waiting it out in Portland. We prayed for the next twelve months, and I continued hoping, despite the economic downturn, for the sale of our house and the good news that would allow me to transfer.

As a side note, in spite of the wait, I thoroughly enjoyed waking up every day, opening the Word, and sending out something fresh for others (including myself) to meditate on. Let me put it this way - living by yourself after 30 years of marriage really gives you time to examine your life, family, relationships, work, or just about anything else that matters. Things begin to take on quite a different perspective. Not that my values were all out of whack - quite the contrary! Priorities began to shift. Some of those things which demanded my attention before began to seem less important.

Backing up for a moment..... Linda and Elisa had optimistically started out in a one bedroom apartment. We all knew this was temporary, right? The mother and daughter relationship was good, but the close quarters put it to the test at times, from what I was told. When Johnny headed South as well, they upsized to a two bedroom. It was still tight. Johnny's stories about those times are pretty funny. Both of the kids were doing great socially, plugging in at church and making friends. My heart went out to Linda as she, being more social than all of us, was in a more difficult place than she had ever been before. With me being so far away, it was hard for her to get connected. She wasn't single but couldn't really hang with married couples either. Her work had its own unique set of circumstances to navigate, and her best friend, me, wasn't there to hold her when I knew she was hurting. So I bought her a puppy. Funny as that may seem, it was great fun and a much needed distraction. We emailed pictures back and forth of all kinds of four legged companions. We ended up with an adorable, Yorkiepoo. Since he was a "he" and strutted with the confidence of a man, we named him Manhe. Just a quick side note, we used to have a girl dog who was a "her" and a "she," and we called her "Hershey." What a blessing the little guy turned out to be for my Sweetie. Later, they moved yet another time to a three bedroom condo type apartment. This gave them all some breathing room and felt more like a home. After owning a home for thirty plus years, renting was, to say the least, uncomfortable. Elisa loved her position at the church. Johnny rose to the top of sales in his first month in Texas, became an assistant store manager, and later took a sales position with a well known roofing company and has done very well.

In January 2009, out of the blue, Linda's elderly father had a major stroke and was found alone in his home after five terrifying hours. She caught the first flight out to Portland and stood in amazement beside her father, realizing this could have taken his life. Instead, it was apparent that he would, with some time and rehab, be back to his old self. I don't believe this trip was a coincidence. Linda was home with me the next morning when I received a call from my company to attend a meeting downtown. They had begun their annual reorganization, and I was hopeful that today would be the day for me. As I was leaving, I gave Linda a hug. She said something rather unusual. You see, she is usually the positive one, but this time she cautiously said, "John, I hope they give you the job, but just in case that's not why they have called you, I want you to know I felt like the Lord assured me that He will take care of us - regardless." I appreciated her support but kind of dismissed it as I continued to my appointment. This reorganization included a downsize typical of the economic times as this decade came to a close.

Instead of finding me a position, they informed me that they were letting me go. Linda was not surprised when I returned home with the news and left me alone to work through the emotions and reality of what just occurred. After about an hour I came downstairs and announced..... I am FREE! Not only was I free from the politics of my corporate position, but I was also free to move and reunite our family, neither of us could stop smiling. Since her Dad was doing so well and had other family members to assist him, there was nothing holding us back. In the next four days we sold, packed, and gave away what wouldn't fit in the largest U-haul we could rent. We left our house clean and empty, and off we went, happy as two larks. We had a blast bouncing (I mean it...U-hauls bounce) across the country. We laughed and totally enjoyed each precious hour together...finally. By the way, in case you are wondering, in the following 12 months, Linda's father made remarkable progress. He even got his driver's license restored at 86—a little scary, but he's an amazing guy! The move started a new chapter in our lives, one of which included the addition of two new family members. Elisa met the man of her dreams, Ben, and they were married in May 2010. Not long after that, wedding bells were ringing for Johnny and his sweet wife Tara. We love them like our own.

WRAP UP

This book is designed as a fun and practical way to get us into the greatest book ever written, the Bible. The goal is to use it as the author intended: to build yourself up, for encouragement, and to get direction, instruction, and comfort.

I know I briefly discussed how I started Daddy Devo's, but I'd like to take a moment to expound yet again on the reason I began to do it in the first place. I was sitting in my recliner doing my daily reading of the Word when the thought came in my mind, "Why don't you use your daily reading as something to encourage the whole family." I opened to the book of Proverbs, and I began to weep. I tend to do this when I feel the Spirit of God come over me. The family, the family, the family," were the words which kept reverberating over and over in my head. I needed to find some way to encourage my family. It wasn't something that was to be a onetime occurrence. No, not one time, but a daily text that combines scripture and a thought or quip for the day. Day after day, I sent them out, and it wasn't until a couple of months went by that I truly realized what the Lord was up to. I hadn't missed a day, to that point, when Linda and I were on our daily call, and she described the affect my Daddy Devo's were having on all of them in Texas. She went on and on about how much she and the kids appreciated knowing that her husband and their dad cared enough to cover them each day with prayer and an encouraging word. It brought a tangible, visible expression of my love for them out of the heavens and into the real world. Linda continued by saying how secure it made them all feel, especially during this extremely vulnerable time.

I want to be transparent here, there was a time in my life when I wasn't doing what I knew was my responsibility as the head of my household. I never stopped reading and praying myself, but what I've come to realize is that apathy doesn't just all of sudden appear out of nowhere. It subtly creeps in over a period of time and gradually takes over, and you don't even know it happened. I had reached that point when God captured my attention. It was at the beginning of this whole ordeal you've been reading about that I felt something stir deep inside of me. My family needed me. So I made the transition from an apathetic man sitting back and letting life do the dictating to a man of action, reigning in his life and becoming the son that God wanted me to be.

All that, folks, came out of a few minutes sincerely spent with the Lord each day. OK, let's get started. I've provided the words for you less adventurous souls out there. I encourage you to pray over each and every word and to allow God to use you in creative ways to minister to your family. Thank you so much for reading this, and I can't wait to hear how God uses you in transforming your life, family, and community.

DADDY DEVO'S
Let the transformation begin.

Some brief instructions before you start:

1. Have your Bible handy. If you don't have a Bible, get one or call me, and I'll give you one.
2. Open your Bible to the scripture for each day.
3. Read the **context** in which the scripture is found.
4. Pray over the scripture or portion.
5. Create a group **Text:** on your phone or whatever electronic device you have. If you don't **Text,** I suggest you learn how! It's always inspiring to learn something new. Besides, how will they get to their desired destination if you don't? Send the **Text!**
6. Or you can sit down with your family if you can get them all together consistently. However, most find it a necessity with our fast-paced society, to follow number 5.
7. You may do it manually should you choose. There is no right or wrong way to do this; the main point of it is that you do it at all.

The following 365 scriptures are ones that I have personally used over the past few years. You are welcome to start with a few of them to get the hang of it or simply use them every day as I did until you develop a habit. I think you'll find them inspirational, humorous, practical, and most of all, a blessing to those whom you choose to send them.

Let me explain my reasoning for the format. The **Text** is the portion which you will actually send via text message. For your benefit, I have added **Key Word**, which breaks down a key word in each text, and **Explanation** to add more meaning and additional application to each day's scripture. Finally, the **Prayer** is for you to pray over yourself and those receiving your text to provide confirmation of the Word for both you and them.

Day 1

Text:
Dd Today: Pr 19 There are many plans in a man's heart, nevertheless the Lord's counsel, that will stand. Who's making your plans? ☺

Key word:
Plan: a scheme or method of acting, doing, proceeding, making, etc., developed in advance: battle plans.

Synonyms: plot, formula, system. Plan, project, design, and scheme imply a formulated method of doing something. Plan refers to any method of thinking out acts and purposes beforehand

Explanation:
As we make our plans, we should always consult the Lord before entering into them, for as our scripture says, ultimately it is the Lord's counsel that will establish, affirm, or direct our plans.

Prayer:
Lord, thank You for giving us the freedom to make plans and help us to be sensitive to the leading of Your Spirit in carrying them out. Amen

Day 2

Text:
Dd Today: Mat 17 Unbelief can paralyze us, if you have the faith of a mustard seed you may speak to a mtn & it will move. Lord, help our unbelief. 😊

Key word:
Unbelief: the state or quality of not believing; incredulity or skepticism, esp. in matters of doctrine or religious faith. "absence or lack of religious belief"

Matthew Henry says: "It is because of our unbelief, that we bring so little to pass in religion, and so often miscarry, and come short, in that which is good. Our Lord Jesus takes this occasion to show them the power of faith, that they might not be defective in that, another time, as they were now; *If ye have faith as a grain of mustard-seed*, ye shall do wonders,"...it refers to the quantity; "If you had but a grain of true faith, though so little that it were like that which is the least of all seeds, you would do wonders."

Explanation:
It isn't in the complete quality of our belief which activates an action on behalf of the Lord. It happens in the moment we exercise the minutest quantity of believing that He steps in and takes it to the next level.

Prayer:
As the disciples prayed out of understanding the importance of not only believing in You but knowing Your heart is to move on our stepping out in the smallest of faith moments to grant our requests. Thank you, Lord, for understanding our frailties and believing in us in spite of them. Amen.

Day 3

Text:
Dd Today: Pr 18 Tells us the words of a tale bearer are like tasty trifles, going down into the in most body. What words do we feast on? ☺

Key word:
Words: a unit of language, consisting of one or more spoken sounds or their written representation that functions as a principal carrier of meaning.
Synonyms: statement, declaration, pledge, message, report, account

Explanation:
We've all heard the "sticks and stones" line and have experientially had a much different result. Words are powerful and can bring about some remarkable consequences both positive and negative. Therefore choosing our words is a very important element in communicating. Also, the words we allow ourselves to see and dwell on will only come out at the most inappropriate times. 'Out the mouth the heart speaks'.

Prayer:
Let the words of my mouth and the meditations of my heart be acceptable in Your sight, oh Lord.

Day 4

Text:
Dd Today: Mat 12 Jesus tells us that a good man out of the good treasure of his heart brings forth good things & a bad man quite the opposite. And our heart? ☺

Key word:
Heart: Physically: The chambered muscular organ in vertebrates that pumps blood received from the veins into the arteries, thereby

maintaining the flow of blood through the entire circulatory system.

Psychologically: The repository of one's deepest and sincerest feelings and beliefs

Spiritually: The heart is the centre not only of spiritual activity, but also of all the operations of human life. The heart is also the seat of the conscience and the true essence of who we really are.

Explanation:
As with the planting of seed, we need to keep the soil free of anything that could harm the growth and maturing of our crop. The Bible refers to our heart as earth or soil, and as the crop we sow in the natural ground, so it is with our heart. We are continually in the process of weeding, fertilizing, and cultivating our character crop.

Prayer:
Father, make me keenly aware and super sensitive to anything that would take away from the growing and cultivating of a good crop in the garden of my heart. Amen

Day 5

Text:
Dd Today: Mat 11 Jesus tells us to come to Him, all who labor & are heavy laden & I will give you rest...for My yoke is easy & My burden is light. Are we willing? 😊

Explanation:
Jesus said, "All who ARE heavy laden," not those who might be. James puts it this way, "WHEN you encounter various trials," not IF you encounter them. The key here is will we come willingly. After all, we are not puppets on a string, and He much prefers it that way. If we will freely come, He will freely offer His assistance in carrying even the heaviest of burdens. It is very much like pumping iron all day, and then someone offering you a feather.

Prayer:
I come to You, Lord, with all my humanity just dripping with the sweat of life and the intricacies thereof. Please place Your yoke on me where we can weather this heavy load together. Amen

Day 6

Text:
Dd Today: Mat 9 Tells us of the woman who pursued Jesus thru the crowd, just so she could touch the hem of His garment. Do we have such perseverance? ☺

Key word:
Perseverance: steady persistence in a course of action, a purpose, a state, etc., esp. in spite of difficulties, obstacles, or discouragement.

Synonyms: doggedness, steadfastness. PERSEVERANCE, PERSISTENCE, TENACITY, and PERTINACITY imply resolute and unyielding holding on in following a course of action.

Explanation:
In our pursuit of Jesus, no matter what we are seeking, whether it be healing, counsel, wisdom, etc., are we relentless like Jacob wrestling with the angel till he blessed him? Hang on and don't let go. If you ask your father for bread, does he give you a stone? Of course not, and our Lord is much more gracious than our earthly fathers.

Prayer:
Lord, I come to you with the perseverance of Jacob. Until You bring about a change in my circumstances, health, finances, relationships, _____, I will pursue You for an answer. Open my eyes and ears to recognize and understand it when it comes. Amen

Day 7

Text:
Dd Today: Mat 7 Ask (insistent asking) & it will be given to you, seek & you will find, knock & it will be opened to you. We must never cease doing all 3. 😊

Explanation:
Asking, seeking, and knocking are rewarded throughout the Bible. I think it's obvious that right motives and humility go hand in hand with these requests, but the one thing we can count on is He turns a deaf ear to us and will always answer us. Not always in the way we would like, but remember His ways are not our ways and His answer will be for our good.

Prayer:
Lord, examine my heart, and if there be any wicked in me, reveal it to me that together we can work through the cleansing process. Now I come to You asking Your blessing and protection on my family, seeking Your favor and Your perfect will for my life, knocking that You may open doors that will propel me and my family into days of prosperity. Amen

Day 8

Text:
Dd Today: Pr 13 Tells us hope deferred makes the heart sick, but when desire comes, it is a tree of life. Let's put our expectations in Him & eat at the tree. 😊

Key word:
Expectation: the act or state of looking forward or anticipating; a prospect of future good or profit; the degree of probability that something will occur.
Synonyms: expectancy, anticipation; hope, trust.

Explanation:
The one thing about putting our expectations in Christ is we can never set them too high. We all know what happens when we put our expectations in a person, place, or thing. The more we put our hope and trust in the Lord, the more hope and trust He will put in us.

Prayer:
My hope is nothing less than Jesus' blood and righteousness. As I approach each day, Lord, I will continually place my expectations, hope, and trust in You. Give me enough wisdom for today, enough creativity for tomorrow, and enough common sense to make it all work. Amen

Day 9

Text:
Dd Today: Pr 12 Anxiety in the heart of a man causes depression, but a good word makes it glad. With our words, let us disperse anxiety. ☺

Key Word:
Disperse - to drive or send off in various directions; scatter; to dispel; cause to vanish
Synonyms: scatter, diffuse, dislodge, disappear.

Explanation:
As we go about our day, we have the ability and influence to change the atmosphere around us. Whether at work, home, or play, what we speak can and will affect the attitude of those who come into contact with us. Make a commitment to lighten the air with a few good words every day.

Prayer:
As I go about my everyday tasks, Lord, bring to my mind good words, words that will change the atmosphere around me and scatter, diffuse, and dislodge any anxiety that may try to raise its ugly head. Amen

Day 10

Text:
Dd Today: Lam 3 Through the Lord's mercies we are not consumed, because His compassions fail not. They are new every morning. Let's look past our circumstances. ☺

Key Word:
cir·cum·stancecircumstance: a condition, fact, or event accompanying, conditioning, or determining another
Synonyms: occurrence, event, incident, episode occurrence, event, incident, episode

Explanation:
Fortunately our lives are not determined by our circumstances but how we react or respond to them. "Remember: Happiness is not a desitination; it's just a method of travel." Red Skelton

Prayer:
Father, as I look at what is transpiring around me, open my eyes to see beyond those things which so easily slow me down and listen to those thoughts that propel me forward. Amen

Day 11

Text:
Dd Today: Pr 10 The blessing of the Lord makes rich, He adds no sorrow with it. Let us be mindful & note his blessings regularly. Sorrow minimized! ☺

Key word:
sorrow: resultant unhappy or unpleasant state; a cause of grief or sadness
Synonyms: grief, anguish, woe, regret mean distress of mind

Explanation:
There must be something to the old adage of 'counting your blessings' because as we do, our troubles seem to fade from view. Abraham certainly took the opportunity, and in blessing, he blessed others.

Prayer:
Lord, there are so many things to be thankful for. Help me to recognize your faithfulness each and every day and to impart it to others along the way. Amen

Day 12

Text:
Dd Today: Ps 8 O Lord our Lord, how excellent is Your name in all the earth. You have given us dominion over all You made. Let us act appropriately. ☺

Key word:
Appropriate: especially suitable or compatible; fitting

Explanation:
I think some of us need to be reminded that He gave us dominion over this planet in the very beginning, not the reverse.

Prayer:
In all my thoughts, words, and actions, make me keenly aware of Your giving me dominion over my thoughts, words and actions. Amen

Day 13

Text:
Dd Today: Pr 8 Wisdom speaks of excellent things, from her lips come right things, for her mouth will speak truth. Are your ears tingling? ☺

Key word:
Tingle: to feel a ringing, stinging, prickling, or thrilling sensation
Synonyms: thrill, flutter

Explanation:
A lot of the time, we are so preoccupied with the things of life that we simply don't settle ourselves long enough to hear what's really going on all around us. As we allow ourselves the pleasure of a quiet few moments, it will surprise us the volumes there at our disposal.

Prayer:
Shhhhhhhh! Let Him do the talking....

Day 14

Text:
Dd Today: Pr 7 Tells us to keep His law & live, we are to call wisdom & understanding our nearest kin. Imagine: a relative that isn't a distraction. 😊

Key word:
Kin: a person's relatives collectively; kinfolk; a group of persons descended from a common ancestor or constituting a family, clan, tribe, or race.
Synonyms: affinity, blood, clan, connection

Explanation:
Focusing in on what He deems important gives us a companion who consistently gives solid counsel and direction. Never once does the Word lead us astray, for it always helps us to find our way.

Prayer:
There are many ways in which You speak to us, but Your word is the most consistent. Give us a desire to devour Your book as if it were going to be our last meal. Amen

Day 15

Text:
Dd Today: Ps 16 You will show me the path of life, in Your presence is fullness of joy. Invade His presence and He will invade yours. ☺

Key word:
Joy: often attributed to or associate with gladness, brightness, to shine always in the context of coming from the Lord, in His presence is fullness of Joy.
Synonyms: gladness, mirth, elation, peace

Explanation:
There is a place we can go where we will only walk away changed and filled with His calm, His peace, His comfort, His rest, and ultimately His joy.

Prayer:
When we are faithful to take time away from our busy schedules, sweep us off our business and into the place where only joy and peace reside. Amen

Day 16

Text:
Dd Today: Jer 42 Cautions us not to come to the Lord under false pretenses, wrong motives, or hypocritically. Let's come to Him with a pure heart, blameless. ☺

Key word:
Blameless: free from or not deserving blame
Synonyms: irreproachable, innocent

Explanation:
David said, "Create in me a clean heart, oh Lord." Remember David was far from sinless, but he was above all blameless.

Prayer:
There is that place, Lord, in which Your view overshadows all other perspectives. It is there that we wish to come, offering ourselves to you a living sacrifice, blameless before You. Amen

Day 17

Text:
Dd Today: Pr 4 Says hear my son(daughter) & receive my sayings & the years of your life will be many. Let's make our years long and prosper, listen. 😊

Key word:
Hear: to receive information by the ear or otherwise
Synonyms: attend, regard, heed, listen

Explanation:
There are times when we hear but are not listening, and we seem to be listening but are having trouble hearing. When coupled together, the two bring revelation.

Prayer:
As we calm ourselves before You, Lord, open our ears that we may hear with a listening ear, always perceiving and understanding the words we are hearing. Amen

Day 18

Text:
Dd Today: Pr 2 We are to seek wisdom, knowledge, discernment & understanding as we would silver or hidden treasure. Shouldn't we seek Him in the same manner? 😊

Key word:
Seek: To try to locate or discover; search for
Synonyms: pursue, follow

Explanation:
When we seek or pursue something or someone, we normally have a definite purpose or intent in doing so. In this case, seeking the Lord as hidden treasure intensifies the emotion and reward of having apprehended our goal.

Prayer:
As we lay out before You and press toward the mark of the Your high calling, seeking You with all our heart, honor us, oh Lord, and meet with us. Amen

Day 19

Text:
Dd Today: Jer 35 Says the Rechabites, because they obeyed the commands of their father, would not lack a man to stand before God. Obey God? Let's see, uh, OK. 😊

Key word:
Obey: to comply with or follow (a command, restriction, wish, instruction, etc.). to submit or conform in action to (some guiding principle, impulse, one's conscience, etc.).
Synonyms: submit, conform, carry out

Explanation:
We must first know the commands of our Father, then act on them. It is lack of obedience that caused sin to come into the world, and obedience that will bring blessing back into it.

Prayer:
There are many things in life that give us opportunity to learn the blessing of obedience. Lord, never let us look beyond those opportunities, but be ever mindful that they are always right before us. Amen

Day 20

Text:
Dd Today: Pr 30 Every word of the Lord is pure & He is a shield to those who trust in Him. Do you trust Him enough to be your shield today, every day? 😊

Key word:
Trust: reliance on the integrity, strength, ability, surety, etc., of a person or thing; confidence; to permit to remain or go somewhere or to do something without fear of consequences

Synonyms: certainty, belief, faith. Trust, assurance, and confidence imply a feeling of security.

Explanation:
The question we have to ask ourselves consistently is if we really trust that God is who He says He is and that He will truly be our shield. All this without fear of consequences should we do something contrary to or violating that trust.

Prayer:
Today, Lord, I put down my defenses long enough to expose myself to Your ultimate protecting shield. I allow You to put Your armor on me. Amen

Day 21

Text:
Dd Today: Jer 31 Our souls will be like a well-watered garden...that the virgin, young & old shall dance, our mourning turned to joy. Shall we dance? 😊

Key word:
Dance: to leap, skip, etc., as from excitement or emotion
Synonyms: cavort, caper, frolic, gambol, prance

Explanation:
As we move through life, the Lord will choose to fill us over and over again with His Holy Spirit, causing our souls to be like a well-watered garden flourishing and quickening our physical bodies to the point of wanting to dance for the joy of it.

Prayer:
There are few moments that I can be describe as being overwhelmed, elated, ecstatic, bursting with energy, and those would be when You fill me with Your Holy Spirit. Peter described it as being filled again and again and again. Thank You, Lord, for filling us again and again and again. Amen

Day 22

Text:
Dd Today: Pr 28 A faithful man-one who is firm, sure, established, conscientious, certain & steady, will abound in blessings. Michieli amplified ver. ☺

Key word:
Abound: to be rich or well supplied
Origins: overflow, run over, rise in a wave

Explanation:
The Lord is looking for a few faithful men, men He can trust, and He will be faithful to make sure that we abound, overflow, run over, and rise in a wave of blessings. Faithful is all He asks.

Prayer:
Teach us Lord to be faithful men and women of God, always leaning on You. When we do waver, teach us to throw in our lot with You, for when we are weak, then You are found strong. Amen

Day 23

Text:
Dd Today: Jude tells us to build ourselves up on your most holy faith, praying in the HS. Let us not minimize the power there is in our Helper. Speak it out. ☺

Key word:
Power: great or marked ability to do or act; strength; might; force; Biblical reference is to the force of dynamite
Synonyms: capacity, energy, strength

Explanation:
There is a time for everything under heaven, but now, the present, daily is the time to build ourselves up in our most holy faith. The times we live in warrant it more than ever before, so speak it out boldly and let the power of the Spirit of the Living God show itself.

Prayer:
Our world is moving at such blazing speed these days, so we ask You, Lord, to help us use our heavenly language to calm the moment and bring sanity in a time of ever-increasing need for wise decisions. Pour out Your Spirit on us, thank You. Amen

Day 24

Text:
Dd Today: 1 Jn 5 We can have confidence in Him, if we ask anything according to His will, He hears us & grants us our request. Never cease to ask. ☺

Key word:
Grants: to agree or accede to
Synonyms: award, vouchsafe, give

Explanation:
We can always trust that He will give us the desires of our heart. The key is in the asking, and He is ever willing and waiting to grant us our requests.

Prayer:
Lord, we trust that You are a Father who is more than willing to grant us our petitions. If our earthly fathers know how to give us good gifts, how much more will You, our heavenly Father, give us the desires of our heart? Amen

Day 25

Text:
Dd Today: 1 Jn 4 He who is in you is greater than he who is in the world. Is He in you? How much? ☺

Key word:
Greater: being superior, transcendent, better than great
Synonyms: superior, transcendent

Explanation:
Peter spoke of being filled with the Holy Spirit over and over and over again as more of an ongoing process. In this sense, we are constantly being endowed with power to overcome the world. All we need do is step outside of our everyday box and let Him in.

Prayer:
There are many things this world has to offer, but none of them even comes close in comparison with the power, insight, sensitivity, etc. that happens when we are filled with the Holy Spirit. As we offer ourselves to You, Lord, fill us again and again with the overcoming power that You experienced at Your rising. Quicken us, Lord, even us. Amen.

Day 26

Text:
Dd Today: Prov 24 Though a righteous man fall 7 times, yet he will rise again. There are many times when we feel like giving in, Yet We Will Rise. ☺

Key word:
Rise: to get up after falling or being thrown down, to return from the dead
Synonyms: arise, proceed, mount, succeed, advance.

Explanation:
The whole fact of it is that we are going to make mistakes. How we respond to those mistakes is the key to living our lives. Christ rose from the dead, but He's not asking us to rise from the dead, only our dead thinking.

Prayer:
We know and can be assured that we will fall, but shake us up, Lord, so that we will shake off the apathetic spirit of dead thinking and rise to the occasion. Thank You, Amen.

Day 27

Text:
Dd Today: 2 Pet 3 Stir up your pure minds by way of reminder, that you be mindful of the words spoken before by the prophets. Let's read the Word. ☺

Key word:
Mindful: attentive, aware, or careful
Synonyms: heedful, thoughtful, regardful

Explanation:
There are so many times I have looked back and been so thankful that I read the Word every day. It has truly been a stabilizing influence in my life, safely grounding me in principles that I only get from The Book.

Prayer:
As we are faithful to open Your book, Lord, show us Your faithfulness by illuminating its meaning to us through, helping us apply it to our everyday lives. Amen.

Day 28

Text:
Dd Today: Jer 18 shows us how we are like a clay vessel in the Potter's hand. He makes it, breaks it & remakes it to His design. Let's get on & stay on His wheel. ☺

Key word:
Remake: anything that has been remade, renovated, or rebuilt

Explanation:
In this case the remaking is usually a voluntary action we submit to; however, we may or may not know the remaking is taking place until we experience the finished product. Contrary to when we remake something, He always makes it better the second time around, that is if we'll stay on the wheel long enough.

Prayer:
In everything we do, Lord, make us cognizant of Your hand upon us and the working of the Holy Spirit in making the individual You would have us to be. Amen

Day 29

Text:
Dd Today: 1 Pet 5 God resists the proud, but gives grace to the humble. Let us do the humbling before He gets to it first. ☺

Key word:
Humble: not proud or arrogant; modest, **courteously respectful**, to make meek
Synonyms: unpretending, unpretentious, submissive, meek, unassuming, plain, common, poor, polite

Explanation:
In a day when pride in just about anything is exalted, especially in one's self, God has not changed His point of view. He still sees us in the light of the Truth that says the first shall be last and those to be revered are the servants among us.

Prayer:
As we go about our daily activities, heighten our sensitivity to those opportunities to serve, coming under and pushing everyone around us to the top, for if we are successful in making them successful, we are successful. Amen

Day 30

Text:
Dd Today: Pr 20 The spirit of a man is the lamp of the Lord, searching all the inner depths of his heart. Search us oh Lord. ☺

Key word:
Search: to look at or examine (a person, object, etc.) carefully in order to find something concealed
Synonyms: investigate, inspect, inspection, scrutiny

Explanation:
We are a many-faceted being, and we love to tuck away little things that we want no one to know or think might be there. We can be experts in disguise and, like Jacob, tend toward deceit rather than openness.

Prayer:
When David prayed, "Search me oh God and know my heart," he was absolutely sincere in every word. With ultimate sincerity I ask you, oh Lord, to search me and see if there be any wicked in me. Try me and know my inward thoughts. Amen

Day 31

Text:
Dd Today: Pr 21 There is no wisdom or understanding or counsel against the Lord. Who are you listening to? ☺

Key word:
Listen: to give attention with the ear; attend closely for the purpose of hearing; give ear
Synonyms: hear

Explanation:
There have been many times I have caught myself listening to thoughts that were obviously not from above. I have to take into captivity those thoughts and only allow my thoughts to be those of Phil 4 – good, lovely, pure, good report, etc.

Prayer:
Give ear to our prayer, oh Lord, and as we put our ears in listening mode, speak ever so loudly and clearly with wisdom, understanding, and counsel. Amen

Day 32

Text:
Dd Today: Mat 20, Jesus tells us that He did not come to be served, but to serve, give, lay down His life. Let's improve our serve & require less service. ☺

Key word:
Serve: To be of assistance to or promote the interests of *another before your own(my addition)*
Synonyms: attend, aid

Explanation:
In looking for ways to assist, attend to, aid or promote the interests of others, we will not only help them succeed, but in so doing, will lose ourselves and thus take up our cross with Him who bore it in the first place.

Prayer:
Lord, there is a place where we can go that supersedes us and allows room for those who really matter. Take us to that place and never let us go. Amen

Day 33

Text:
Dd Today: Pr 21 It is a joy for the just to do justice, but it terrifies evildoers. It is good for the good to do good, the bad rage against it. ☺

Key word:
Rage: to act or speak with fury; show or feel violent anger; fulminate
Synonyms: wrath, frenzy, passion, ire, madness

Explanation:
The ire of the evil one is intensified when we do good, promote righteousness, justice, and every pure thing. To stand for what is right- what a novel concept.

Prayer:
Open our spiritual eyes, Lord, to see beyond the bad and focus on the good in every person, situation, and circumstance. Amen

Day 34

Text:
Dd Today: Pr 22 A sterling reputation is better than striking it rich. We are not responsible for what others think of us, only to not give them a case. 😊

Key word:
Sterling: thoroughly excellent
Synonyms: noble, honorable, worthy, first-rate.

Explanation:
It is only when our reputation slips away that we realize what we had in the first place, which brings great meaning to the saying, you never get a second chance to make a first impression.

Prayer:
Lord, we are not responsible for what others think of us; You are. Always keep us well aware of what we can do to keep them from those thoughts. Amen

Day 35

Text:
Dd Today: Pr 23 My son, give me your heart & let your eyes observe my ways. As we open our heart to Him, He will show us where & what we should do. ☺

Key word:
Observe: to see, watch, perceive, or notice, to regard with attention, esp. so as to see or learn something
Synonyms: witness

Explanation:
If you really want to know where and what you should do, be sure and include Him all the time. He's there anyway; why not let Him be involved.

Prayer:
Always remind us that You have eyes and ears in every place, orchestrating, choreographing, wooing us by Your Spirit. Open our eyes to Your possibilities. Amen

Day 36

Text:
Dd Today: Pr 24 By wise counsel you will wage your own war & in a multitude of counselors is safety. We limit our strength by limiting our advisors. ☺

Key word:
Limit: to restrict by or as if by establishing limits
Synonyms: confine, restrain, bound

Explanation:
Being in a war requires us to have a strategy. Planning without wise counsel limits our ability to succeed.

Prayer:
In our ever-churning Spiritual battle, we look to You, our ultimate counselor, to keep us focused on the task at hand, enhancing our progression toward success. Amen

Day 37

Text:
Dd Today: Pr 25 Whoever has no rule over his/her own spirit is like a city broken down w/out walls. Self control is protection to those who use it. ☺

Key word:
Protection: the act of protecting or the state of being protected; preservation from injury or harm
Synonyms: security, refuge, safety. guard, defense, shield, bulwark

Explanation:
We all know that a city without walls in Old Testament times was totally vulnerable and completely unprotected. Exactly how we are when we don't use self control.

Prayer:
Teach us the art of self control throughout our daily lives, continually focusing on the things that truly matter and discarding those that don't. Amen

Day 38

Text:
Dd Today: Mat 25 Jesus tells us that if we are faithful w/the talents He gives us, then we will be rewarded. What are you doing w/your talent(s)? ☺

Key word:
Talent: a power of mind or body considered as given to a person for use and improvement

Synonyms: capability, gift, genius

Explanation:
Many of us go through life dripping with talents and gifts never used or used so infrequently the dust has to be blown off to recognize them. Then there are those who find, develop, and fine tune theirs to an extraordinary level, bravo!

Prayer:
We all know we have been given gifts and talents; challenge us, Lord, to use them to their fullest and not hide them in the recesses of heart only to be brought out on special occasions. Amen

Day 39

Text:
Dd Today: Pr 27 A satisfied stomach can't stand the thought of eating, but one who is hungry even the bitter seems sweet. Are we feasting or fasting? 😊

Key word:
Fasting: A period of such abstention or self-denial
Original meaning: firm control of oneself

Explanation:
Some of us are so satisfied with our existence that we never reach out to anyone or anything and so full of teaching that we could help hundreds of churches around the world or even our own if we just would.

Prayer:
Oh that we would not just be content where we are at but continually strive to give of ourselves to the betterment of those around us. Amen

Day 40

Text:
Dd Today: Ez 22 God sought for a man among them who would make a wall & stand in the gap before Me on behalf of the land. Are we willing to stand? 😊

Key word:
Stand: to take up or maintain a position or attitude with respect to a person, issue, or the like
Synonyms: abide, stomach, bear

Explanation:
Standing isn't always the most popular thing to do but most necessary as we see in various intervals throughout history. All God needs is a few willing souls, and the victory is at hand.

Prayer:
Freewill allows us to make that stand at Your request. No one ever said it would be easy, but doing nothing never did anything for anyone. Use us Lord. Amen

Day 41

Text:
Dd Today: Mat 28 the last verse, Jesus said, 'I am with you always, even to the end of the age.' If we really believe what He said, then let's act like it. 😊

Key word:
Act: anything done, being done, or to be done; deed; performance, the process of doing
Synonyms: feat, exploit; achievement; transaction; accomplishment

Explanation:
Many of us would like to believe that we believe, but we have a hard time putting action to our beliefs.

Prayer:
Lord, You gave us two legs and only one mouth; help us to act out twice as much as we speak out. Amen

Day 42

Text:
Dd Today: Mk 2 Many questioned Jesus' actions & motives, but He never once lost focus on His purpose. Let's not allow opinions to sway us from His purpose. ☺

Key word:
Opinions: a personal view, attitude, or appraisal

Explanation:
It is His purpose that should drive us to the completion of our purpose because the two are interchangeable.

Prayer:
Always keep ours and Yours ever before us, so our perspective is through Your eyes and not our own. Amen

Day 43

Text:
Dd Today: Mk 3 Jesus takes the opportunity to restore a man's hand in the face of opposition. Sometimes we must do what we know is right regardless of opinion. ☺

Key word:
Right: that which is morally, legally, or ethically proper
Synonyms: morality, virtue, justice, fairness, integrity, equity, rectitude

Explanation:
Right is right is right is right, and situations, opinions and circumstances will never change the importance of adhering to what is right.

Prayer:
Open our eyes, Lord, to what is right and give us the strength to hold on to that which right and true. Amen

Day 44

Text:
Dd Today: Mk 5 & 6 The sick woman simply touched His garment & was healed. Also as many as touched Him were made well. Have you touched Him lately? ☺

Key word:
Touched: moved; stirred
Synonyms: move, strike, stir, melt, soften

Explanation:
Many of us would like to move or stir You into action for us; when the woman above took action and approached Him with sincerity of heart, He had compassion on her.

Prayer:
Stir us up, Lord, to reach out our hand to touch the very hem of Your garment. Amen

Day 45

Text:
Dd Today: Mk 7 Jesus tells us nothing that enters a man from outside can defile him, but the things which come out of him. What's inside you? ☺

Key word:
Enter: to put in or insert, to go to or occupy in order to claim possession of
Antonyms: leave or remove

Explanation:
Being in the techno age, we all know that it isn't the computer's fault, it's the one sitting at the keyboard. Garbage in, garbage out!

Prayer:
We all know we will and do make mistakes, but remind us daily, Lord, to leave or remove our mistakes and to learn from them. Amen

Day 46

Text:
Dd Today: Regardless of our circumstances, David seems to have a grip on his attitude in Ps 9, I WILL be glad & rejoice in You; I WILL sing praise to Your name. 😊

Key word:
Will: determined or sure to, the act or process of using or asserting one's choice; volition
Synonyms: choice, pleasure, disposition, inclination, resolution, decision

Explanation:
There definitely is a time when we need to stir ourselves to do what is right regardless how we feel.

Prayer:
In those times when we don't feel like praising You, Lord, challenge our thinking and stir us to will to do what we know is right. Amen

Day 47

Text:
Dd Today: Mk 11 Jesus tells us whoever says to this mtn be removed & doesn't doubt in his heart, whatever you say will be done. Be careful what you say. ☺

Key word:
Doubt: a feeling of uncertainty about the truth, reality, or nature of something
Synonyms: indecision, irresolution

Explanation:
Doubt is a powerful force and is coupled or related to unbelief. As we press forward, let's muster all the conviction we can and speak with boldness and confidence.

Prayer:
Lord, as the disciples showed us, there were many times in which they couldn't do things because of their lack of faith, unbelief, or doubting. May we be convicted and help our unbelief. Amen

Day 48

Text:
Dd Today: Ez 36 He will give us a new heart & a new spirit, taking out the heart of stone & giving us a heart of flesh. Are we teachable or hardened? ☺

Key word:
Teachable: capable of being instructed
Synonyms: able, amenable, apt, bright, docile, eager, intelligent, qualified, skilled, smart

Explanation:
We have so many opportunities to lay down our ego and to absorb, learn, and humble ourselves, which will make everything from that point so much more meaningful.

Prayer:
Ezekiel had so much insight when he prophesied concerning our hearts. Lord, our desire is for that heart of flesh and not one that is hardened and insensitive. Amen

Day 49

Text:
Dd Today: Ps 119 They that love His word, nothing causes them to stumble. Let's fall in love w/His word again for the very first time. 😊

Key word:
Love: a profoundly tender, passionate affection for
Synonyms: tenderness, fondness, predilection, warmth, passion, adoration

Explanation:
There is simply no other book that can foster so many different experiential happenings, elation, sadness, peace of mind, counsel, practical living, wisdom, knowledge, etc. etc. etc.

Prayer:
Lord, Your word sustains us and living. As we read it again, may the breath that made it alive in the first place be breathed into us. Amen

Day 50

Text:
Dd Today: Pr 8 Whoever listens to wisdom will be blessed. Whoever finds wisdom obtains favor from the Lord. If we want His favor, let's have a listen. ☺

Key word:
Favor: excessive kindness or unfair partiality; preferential treatment
Synonyms: goodwill, present, approve, encourage, help, assist

Explanation:
Often times quieting ourselves is one of the most difficult things we try to do. Try is right, but when we succeed, He is always faithful to speak.

Prayer:
In those times when we settle ourselves to the point of quietness, peak the sensitivity of our ears, so we are careful to hear the calmness of Your voice. Amen

Day 51

Text:
Dd Today: Mk 16 Jesus tells us these signs will follow those who believe. In His name..... we will lay hands on the sick & they will recover. Do we believe? ☺

Key word:
Believe: to have confidence or faith in the truth, to have confidence in the truth, the existence, or the reliability of something
Synonyms: trust, be certain of, be convinced of

Explanation:
How many times have we sat down to pray for someone and had that mental hiccup, "I'm going to pray, but I really don't think this person is going to be healed." Well, Stop it!!

Prayer:
Reaffirm our confidence in You, Lord, as we lay it on the line, reaching out, stepping out on the precipice of unknowing, show up. Amen

Day 52

Text:
Dd Today: Ps 42 David remembers the Lord in the middle of a hard time. My soul thirsts for God, for the living God. As a deer pants for water. Are we thirsty? ☺

Key word:
Thirst: To have a strong craving; yearn
Synonyms: eagerness, desire, longing, passion, yearning

Explanation:
Many of us have been in that same place as David, yearning for God to do something, anything, to show us that He is. The fact is, He is, and the thirstier we are, the greater the fulfillment when He grants us the desires of our heart.

Prayer:
In that dry and parched place, come Lord, with the water of which we will never thirst again. Amen

Day 53

Text:
Dd Today: Pr 12 Anxiety in the heart of a man causes depression, but a good word makes it glad. Today let your words be a gift & seal them w/a :). ☺

Key word:
Glad: characterized by or showing cheerfulness, joy, or pleasure, as looks or utterances
Synonyms: merry, joyous, joyful, cheerful, happy, cheery

Explanation:
Anxious moments, we all have them, but if we can assist somehow in making them less by turning up the corners of our mouth and giving an encouraging word, then so be it.

Prayer:
Let the words of our mouth and meditations of our heart be acceptable in Your sight, oh Lord. Amen

Day 54

Text:
Dd Today: Lk 5 Tells us of 4 fishermen who had caught nothing, but when Jesus asked them to cast their nets once more, they're catch was huge. Never doubt Him. ☺

Key word:
Cast: to throw off or away, to look, as to find something; search; seek
Synonyms: throw, turn

Explanation:
In asking them to throw their nets in a different direction, knowing who He was dealing with, Jesus was instantly proving their trust and belief or, as it were, their unbelief.

Prayer:
How many times have we been going one direction only to find out we needed to turn around and cast our nets in His direction? Show us Your direction, Lord. Amen

Day 55

Text:
Dd Today: Pr 15 A soft answer turns away wrath, but a harsh word stirs up anger. Look anger in the face and give what you know it doesn't want. ☺

Key word:
Soft: low or subdued in sound; gentle and melodious, smooth, soothing, or ingratiating
Synonyms: mellifluous, dulcet, sweet, tender, sympathetic

Explanation:
So many times and occasions come and go in which we have the opportunity to lash out in answer to some superfluous comment. Since we do have a choice, choose to be mellifluous.

Prayer:
Lord, help us to always respond and not react without thinking. Amen

Day 56

Text:
Dd Today: Lk 6 Jesus tells us not to judge or condemn, but forgive & we will be forgiven. Give & it will be given to you. Giving in all things will be rewarded. ☺

Key word:
Giving: to present voluntarily and without expecting compensation; bestow
Synonyms: impart, accord, furnish, provide, supply, donate, contribute

Explanation:
We can always give our way out of trouble, but we can never take our way out trouble.

Prayer:
Our consistency is a must when it comes to giving. Always remind us that we can never ever out give You. Amen

Day 57

Text:
Dd Today: Lk 8 The sower went out & sowed seed, some by the wayside, some on the rocks, some among thorns & some on good grnd. How's your soil? 😊

Key word:
Sow: to implant, introduce, or promulgate; seek to propagate or extend; disseminate
Synonyms: inject, lodge, circulate

Explanation:
I don't think we realize that the Bible is very clear that our heart is like soil, and whatever we sow in our heart is what we will reap in our life. Sown seeds grow, no matter what flavor they are.

Prayer:
To grow a good crop is to know how, what, and when to plant. Cultivate our hearts Lord, that the fruit of our lives be a reflection of You. Amen

Day 58

Text:
Dd Today: Pr 20 The spirit of a man is the lamp of the Lord, searching all the inner depths of his heart. Are we willing to let His light shine? 😊

Key word:
Search: to look at or examine (a person, object, etc.) carefully in order to find something concealed
Synonyms: inspection, scrutiny

Explanation:
While we're constantly inspecting the outside, He is diligently examining the inside, knowing the outside is only a reflection of what's in there.

Prayer:
Create in me a clean heart, oh God. See if there be any wicked in me and create a right spirit within me. Amen

Day 59

Text:
Dd Today: Dan 3 recounts the image the king saw in a dream, even though it was made strong it had feet of clay. We all have feet of clay, but God makes us strong. 😊

Key word:
Strong: solid or stable; healthy; thriving
Synonyms: steady, firm, secure, unwavering, resolute

Explanation:
In all abilities, strengths, talents and gifting, there is always that element we can never escape while here on this earth, our humanity.

Prayer:
We are never at a better place than when we submit our will to Yours, realizing that truly, when we are weak, then You can be strong. Amen

Day 60

Text:
Dd Today: Dan 3 Tells us of Shadrach, Meshach & Abednego being thrown into the fiery furnace for what they believed. God is always faithful if we will stand. 😊

Key word:
Stand: a determined policy, position, attitude, etc., taken or maintained
Synonyms: abide, bear

Explanation:
Taking a stand isn't always the easiest thing to do, but it is then that God seems to be at His best standing beside us.

Prayer:
Never let us forget that we are ever dependent on You and that You will never leave us or forsake us. Amen

Day 61

Text:
Dd Today: Lk 10 Martha complaining that her sister wouldn't help her in her serving, but Jesus said she had chosen the good part. And your choice? 😊

Key word:
Choose: to select from a number of possibilities; pick by preference
Synonyms: select, pick, elect, prefer

Explanation:
We all have the habit of wanting to do, do, do to make sure everything comes out right or at least comfortable instead of using our discernment to choose the best rather than the acceptable.

Prayer:
There are many things which can detract from the core of what would've or could've; show us the power in making the most of the moment, depending on You to gather our focus. Amen

Day 62

Text:
Dd Today: Dan 6 Daniel was falsely accused, thrown in a lion's den & delivered because he believed his God. Do <u>You</u> believe? Our God is Awesome. ☺

Key word:
Believe: to have confidence in the truth, the existence, or the reliability of something, although without absolute proof that one is right in doing so
Synonyms: conceive, consider, think, trust

Explanation:
Very few of us has been exposed to, let alone had to respond to, this kind of accusation. We tend to live with our beliefs at arm's length. We must confront ourselves with the question of do we really believe.

Prayer:
Let it be settled and confirmed in our hearts, the peace that only comes from truly believing. Amen

Day 63

Text:
Dd Today: Lk 12 Jesus says which of you by worrying can add 1 cubit to his stature? Be anxious for nothing, for He <u>cares</u> for you? He Really does! ☺

Key word:
Care: to be concerned or have a special preference
Synonyms: concern, touch, involve

Explanation:
Jesus once said He would never leave us or forsake us, so don't concern yourself with whether or not He cares. Relax, He does.

Prayer:
Take us to a place of understanding which brings us to a point of worry-free concern. Amen

Day 64

Text:
Dd Today: Pr 27 As in water face reflects face, so a man's heart reveals the man. What's your heart condition? 😊

Key word:
Reflect: to give back or show an image of; mirror
Synonyms: manifest, rebound, ruminate, deliberate, muse, consider, cogitate, contemplate

Explanation:
Most times if we'll take a few moments to really examine ourselves, that short reflection shouts to what we are currently experiencing.

Prayer:
With the Word being like a mirror, as we read Your word and see the reflection of who we really are, gently guide us into who You want us to be. Amen

Day 65

Text:
Dd Today: Lk 17, Jesus tells us that if a brother sins against you 7 times a day & comes to you 7 times saying I repent, forgive him. Are you willing? 😊

Key word:
Forgive: to give up resentment of or claim to requital for
Synonyms: pardon, excuse

Explanation:
How many times have we held on to some feeling or resentment toward someone only to have it haunt us until we let them go. It's like the two of you being tangled in a rope, only as forgiveness is issued will the rope begin to release you and your comingling friend.

Prayer:
Lord, grant us the willingness to let go of all unforgiveness so that we may not only release ourselves, but more importantly the offending party, opening us both to Your will and purposes. Amen

Day 66

Text:
Dd Today: Lk 18 Jesus said whoever does not receive the kingdom of God like a little child will by no means enter it. Let's not be childish, but childlike. 😊

Key word:
Like: one that is similar
Synonyms: counterpart, equal

Explanation:
Jesus and Paul were very clear when they wanted us to be like a little child and not be childish. We are to put off childish things and grow up in our faith.

Prayer:
In all Your wisdom, show us how to grow up in our faith without losing that child-like quality You desire. Amen

Day 67

Text:
Dd Today: Lk 19 Jesus tells us that those who can be trusted will be given much, those who can't, theirs shall be taken away. Are we trustworthy? ☺

Key word:
Trustworthy: worthy of confidence
Synonyms: dependable

Explanation:
As we go about our day to day activities, can we be trusted as a steward of those things which are His anyway?

Prayer:
Always remind us that anything we have been given or acquired was originally Yours in the first place and we are to take care of it as such. Amen

Day 68

Text:
Dd Today: Pr 30 God is a shield to those who put their trust in Him. I have to constantly remind myself, where is my trust? Where's yours? ☺

Key word:
Remind: to put in mind of something: cause to remember
Synonyms: remember

Explanation:
Trust is a very big word in a lot of our lives, especially when it comes to trusting someone else. We have a hard enough time trusting ourselves, but that other guy? Hmmm, maybe!!

Prayer:
Wrap Your loving arms around us and show us that we have no fear when it comes to putting our trust, all of our trust, in You. Amen

Day 69

Text:
Dd Today: To seek in Hos 5 is to search earnestly until the object is located, diligently look for. We are to seek the Lord's presence. What are you seeking? ☺

Key word:
Earnestly: characterized by or proceeding from an intense and serious state of mind
Synonyms: grave, important, serious

Explanation:
How many times when we are praying. do we look up at every little sound or movement. When distractions of this sort come, is where the earnest part exists.

Prayer:
In our times with You, Lord, help us to be so focused that nothing can deter or detract from our making contact with You. Amen

Day 70

Text:
Dd Today: Jn 1 in the beginning God spoke the world into existence, He spoke His final word through the living Word. Let's read it again for the very 1st time. ☺

Key word:
Spoke: to make a written statement; to utter words or articulate sounds with the ordinary voice

Synonyms: testify, pronounce, declare, address, state, describe, depict

Explanation:
I was told when I first became a believer that I could not remain one unless I read the Bible every day. That has held true to this very day, 34 years later. Do read it, over and over and over and over again.

Prayer:
I pray that Your word will become equally important as our jobs or hobbies or anything else that we willingly give ourselves to. Amen

Day 71

Text:
Dd Today: Jn 3 Nicodemus being a teacher somehow missed the seals of the covenant mentioned by Jesus, water, spirit, (fire). Are you sealed? ☺

Key word:
Sealed: to affix a seal to in authorization, testimony; used as attestation or evidence of authenticity
Synonyms: impenetrable, fixed, firm

Explanation:
Biblically speaking there are three seals to every covenant: fire, water and spirit. I ask again, are you sealed, saved, water baptized and filled with the Holy Spirit?

Prayer:
Father, I ask that You make real and tangible the three seals of our New Covenant to every one of us so that we may walk out our new-found life with power and confidence, knowing You are who You said You are. Amen

Day 72

Text:
Dd Today: Pr 2 He stores up sound wisdom for the upright & is a shield to those who walk uprightly. What storehouse are you drawing from? 😊

Key word:
Store: quantity, esp. great quantity; abundance, or plenty
Synonyms: vault, accumulation, keep

Explanation:
We usually get to end of our rope before we really tap into what He has stored up for us. Remember He has an unlimited supply. He'll simply make more.

Prayer:
As we walk out our daily lives, show through practical, everyday circumstances how real Your storehouse is and the vastness of it. Amen

Day 73

Text:
Dd Today: Pr 3 Lean not on our own understanding, in all our ways acknowledge Him & He will direct-make straight, right, our paths. Let's lean on Him. 😊

Key word:
Lean: to depend or rely on, count on
Synonyms: bank on, believe in, bet bottom dollar, bet on, <u>confide</u>, have faith

Explanation:
Many of us exhaust all of our possibilities before we ever consider tapping into His. I have definitely had to learn to go to Him first, it just makes sense.

Prayer:
Teach us to truly lean on You instead of ourselves. Amen

Day 74

Text:
Dd Today: Hos 10 To break up your fallow ground, sow righteousness and reap mercy. Lord make our hearts fertile soil. ☺

Key word:
Fallow: land that has undergone plowing and harrowing and has been left unseeded for one or more growing seasons
Synonyms: unproductive, quiescent, uncultivated, dormant, vacant, neglected

Explanation:
Our hearts can become a place of complacency, dormancy, and neglect if we don't allow Him to periodically come in and do a little or a lot of cultivation, fertilization, planting, etc.

Prayer:
Would You break up the fallow ground of our hearts and plant in us a heart that exudes the fruits of the Spirit? Amen

Day 75

Text:
Dd Today: Jn 7 Jesus tells us he who believes in Me, out of his heart will flow rivers of living water. How's your flow, stopped up? Return to the well. ☺

Key word:
Flow: to proceed continuously and smoothly; to abound in something
Synonyms: issue, abundance, effusion, flood, plenty

Explanation:
There are times in our daily lives that we don't feel like getting out of bed, doing the dishes, going to work, mowing the lawn, but thank God we are not to live by our feelings, but by every word that proceeds from His mouth. As we begin to open our mouths in praise, He will fill us again from the well that doesn't run dry.

Prayer:
In those lean times and in times of plenty, show us Your faithfulness as we are faithful to open our hearts before You with the sacrifice of praise from our lips. Amen

Day 76

Text:
Dd Today: Jn 8 as Jesus knelt down to write in the sand, all the woman's accusers left. I wonder what He wrote? What's in your heart? ☺

Key word:
Accuse: to find fault with; blame
Synonyms: slander, apprehend, indict, cite incriminate

Explanation:
We all have various kinds of things we could be accused of, whether it is an action or thought. Jesus just wanted these guys to be accountable, knowing that He knew. He knows!

Prayer:
Lord, we are all subject to wrong thoughts and we know what they are, arrest us in our thinking. Amen

Day 77

Text:
Dd Today: Hos 14 For we will offer the sacrifices (bulls, calves) of our lips. In the OT they sacrificed animals, but today we offer the sacrifice of our lips. ☺

Key word:
Sacrifice: to surrender or give up, for the sake of something else
Synonyms: endure, yield, lose, atonement, offering

Explanation:
We set aside a portion of every church service for praise, but do we really understand the meaning behind sacrificial release of our lips and tongues in offering praise to Him?

Prayer:
Each week and in our personal time, illuminate our minds and hearts as to the power found in our praise. Amen

Day 78

Text:
Dd Today: Jn 9 Jesus spits on the gnd, making clay & putting it on the eyes of a blind man, that he might see. A little mud goes a long way to open our eyes. ☺

Key word:
See: perceive with eyes, appreciate, comprehend
Synonyms: detect, discern, distinguish, ascertain, behold, perceive, take in

Explanation:
Sometimes it takes getting a little mud in our eyes to help us see the actual path we are on so that we can make the necessary navigational corrections.

Prayer:
Do whatever it takes, Lord, to put us on the right path, mud or no. Amen

Day 79

Text:
Dd Today: Pr 20 The godly walk with integrity; blessed are their children who follow them. Remember 2 legs, 1 mouth; we walk twice as much as we talk. ☺

Key word:
Integrity: honor, uprightness
Synonyms: honesty, honorableness, goodness, forthrightness

Explanation:
As we go through life, we don't always realize the vastness of our sphere of influence. Someone is always watching.

Prayer:
Never let us forget the influential person You made us to be. Amen

Day 80

Text:
Dd Today: Jn 11 Jesus calls to Lazarus, come forth! Loose him & let him go. What in our lives do we need Him to loose & let go? ☺

Key word:
Loose: set free; unbind
Synonyms: become unfastened, break up, deliver, disengage

Explanation:
There are many times I have felt all tied up and have wanted to get loose from those ropes. He is the one who can come and untie any knot we may have gotten ourselves into.

Prayer:
Lord, come and set us free from those things which prevent us from moving on. Amen

Day 81

Text:
Dd Today: Joel 2 records an outpouring of the Spirit in which all flesh is affected, daughters, young & old men. Let's be ready in season & out. ☺

Key word:
Ready: prepared; available
Synonyms: adjusted, all set, all systems go, anticipating

Explanation:
Can we prepare for an outpouring of the Spirit? Better yet, is there an outpouring going on or would you even know? Good question.

Prayer:
May we always be prepared for what You want to do with our lives and be willing to do it. Amen

Day 82

Text:
Dd Today: Jn 13 in washing the disciple's feet, Jesus displays the ultimate in serving. Serving comes from the heart & demands action. How's your serve? ☺

Key word:
Serve: aid, help; supply, act, do
Synonyms: attend to, be of assistance, be of use, care for

Explanation:
When I play tennis, my serve can be on and I'm lovin' life; on the other hand, it can be equally as inconsistent.

Prayer:
Help us to drop the inconsistencies of our serving and consistently live a life of service. Amen

Day 83

Text:
Dd Today: Jn 14 Jesus says if we believe in Him, greater works than His will we do. If we ask anything in His name He will do it. Do we believe? Ask!! ☺

Key word:
Ask: request, invite
Synonyms: inquire, hunt for, appeal, contend for

Explanation:
Most times I just go on with life and let things happen as they happen, but what if I was to actually contend for something different? Begin to consistently ask.

Prayer:
Bring out the inquisitiveness in all of us to begin to contend for more fulfillment in our lives. Amen

Day 84

Text:
Dd Today: Pr 13 A man shall eat well by the fruit of his mouth. Just like a balanced diet keeps you healthy, well balanced speech brings peace & life. 😊

Key word:
Balanced: make equal; cause to have equilibrium
Synonyms: accord, adjust, attune, harmonize, level

Explanation:
We've all heard many times that what we say can and will come around to bite us. Well it can also come around and bless us.

Prayer:
Make our words visual statements we can see before we say them. Amen

Day 85

Text:
Dd Today: Amos 7 The Lord set a plumb line (a standard to live by) in the midst of Israel. Let's not live less than the plumb line He has set up for us? 😊

Key word:
Plumb: vertical, probe, go into
Synonyms: erect, straight, upright, measure, gauge

Explanation:
I can't tell you how many times I have looked to the principles in the Word to give me a gauge or measure with which to guide my life.

Prayer:
Show us, Lord, the plumb line You have established. We are not to compare ourselves among ourselves but to look to Your word for guidance. Amen

Day 86

Text:
Dd Today: Pr 17 A merry heart does good like a medicine. Let's give away a few of these -:) :) :) :)-today. ☺

Key word:
Good: pleasant, fine, moral, virtuous, competent, skilled
Synonyms: excellent, exceptional, blameless, ethical, able, accomplished

Explanation:
I can't tell how many times my wife has asked me to give her a smile, and when I do, it brings such satisfaction, peace, and relaxation to her face. Never under estimate the value of turning up the corners of your mouth.

Prayer:
Would You open our understanding of the value You place on others as well as ourselves? Amen

Day 87

Text:
Dd Today: Jonah 2 When we think our circumstances are beyond return, remember Jonah spent 72 hrs inside a fish before his prayer was answered. Pray on!! ☺

Key word:
Circumstances: an unessential or secondary accompaniment of any fact or event; minor detail

Synonyms: action, coincidence, happening, happenstance, incident

Explanation:
There have been many times I have considered myself up against the wall, but when I look at some of our Biblical examples of hard times, I have to adjust my thinking. I'm just not quite there yet.

Prayer:
Lord, You know exactly where we are and what we are going through at any given moment. Open our eyes to see and our ears to hear from a better perspective-Yours. Amen

Day 88

Text:
Dd Today: Acts 2 In response to crowd criticism, Peter was bold & deliberate in his rebut & the church was born. Remember Who is in your court, the Helper? ☺

Key word:
Response: any behavior of a living organism that results from an external or internal stimulus

Synonyms: acknowledgment, respond, comeback, retroaction

Explanation:
How many times have we shrunk back from or simply just not responded to a reaction when in reality the Lord would have us to be bold and speak out?

Prayer:
There is a time to respond and a time to hold our peace. Help us to be bold as lions and meek as lambs as needed. Amen

Day 89

Text:
Dd Today: Acts 3 Peter & John in invoking the full name/title of Jesus Christ of Nazareth, the 1st miracle of Acts is recorded. There is power in using His name. 😊

Key word:
Name: a personal or family name as exercising influence or bringing distinction, a reputation of a particular kind given by common opinion
Synonyms: connote, point to, specify, classify, make

Explanation:
When invoking the name of Jesus over a person or circumstance or event, we are bringing with it all the power and authority linked to it. Using His name is always a good thing to do.

Prayer:
In the name of Jesus we can do all things through Christ who strengthens us. Amen

Day 90

Text:
Dd Today: Pr 18 The name of the Lord is a strong tower, the righteous run into it & are safe. Where do you run when trouble comes? 😊

Key word:
Run: to depart quickly; take to flight; flee or escape
Synonyms: bolt, dart, dash, hasten, hurry

Explanation:
My tendency is to exhaust me before I run to Him. I do everything in MY power, only using God as a last resort. It certainly should be very much the other way around.

Prayer:
Lord, so many times we run to ourselves or others before You. Keep us in the mode to consistently put You first. Seek ye first the kingdom of God and His righteousness. Amen

Day 91

Text:
Dd Today: Jonah 4 Jonah had more regard for a plant than for the redeemed. He was angry over a people who were helplessly lost. God had compassion, do we? ☺

Key word:
Compassion: a feeling of deep sympathy and sorrow for another who is stricken by misfortune, accompanied by a strong desire to alleviate the suffering
Synonyms: commiseration, mercy, tenderness, heart, clemency, empathy

Explanation:
I know I tend to overlook the guy on the street or look past those who are in a difficult situation, or not see them at all, being so concerned with my own circumstance that I tend to be blinded to others. God never sees it that way.

Prayer:
Open our eyes, Lord, to see those You would have us come along side, through prayer, giving, or simply lending a hand. Amen

Day 92

Text:
Dd Today: Pr 19 The discretion of a man makes him slow to anger, & his glory is to overlook a transgression. Forgiveness releases the Lord to work. ☺

Key word:
Discretion: the power or right to decide or act according to one's own judgment; freedom of judgment or choice
Synonyms: judgment, wisdom, discrimination, sense

Explanation:
There are many circumstances in which we have to ignore or overlook what's happening in order to maintain our sanity, especially when dealing with children. They most times will take our lead if we are consistent.

Prayer:
There is a time to speak and a time to keep from speaking. Teach us to use our common sense when confronted with this decision. Amen

Day 93

Text:
Dd Today: Pr 20 The spirit of a man is the lamp of the Lord, searching all the rooms of his belly. Have you cleaned house lately? ☺

Key word:
Cleaned: to remove or consume the contents of; empty; clear
Synonyms: immaculate, pure, unblemished, thoroughly

Explanation:
Sometimes we have to let go and let Him show us just what we need to get rid of. The first step is to give Him complete access to all the closets of our life. Not an easy task, but we all have them, so get the key out.

Prayer:
Open the closets of our heart and use whatever tool is necessary to clean out those hidden corners we hardly ever explore. Amen

Day 94

Text:
Dd Today: Acts 8 Saul persecuted the church throughout the regions & the church was scattered, the word being spread to the known world. Are you relentless? ☺

Key word:
Persecuted: to pursue with harassing or oppressive treatment, esp. because of religion, race, or beliefs; harass persistently
Synonyms: vex, hunt, beat, plague, pursue, afflict

Explanation:
When we are pushed to the edge of our beliefs, do we fold or waffle on our core values? Taking a stand isn't always the easy thing to do, but it is very rewarding.

Prayer:
Lord, You were persecuted to the ultimate limits, and You didn't fold under the pressure but addressed your foes with the Word. Release the HS in us to be bold and to not shrink back. Amen

Day 95

Text:
Dd Today: Acts 9 How many times have we questioned the Lord as Ananias did? Yet in his obedience Saul becomes Paul. Obedience is what brings breakthrough. ☺

Key word:
Breakthrough: any significant or sudden advance, development, achievement, or increase that removes a barrier to progress
Synonyms: advance, progress, leap,

Explanation:
I remember a time when the Lord asked me to return to my parents' house; it took several miles for me to relent with the questioning and just do it. My Dad got saved as a result. Just Do It!

Prayer:
Lord, help us to keep it simple even if we are acting out shear obedience and faith. Amen

Day 96

Text:
Dd Today: Micah 7 emphasizes God's immense compassion & His will to forgive & forget sin, who is a God like You, pardoning iniquity. Praise God for His mercy on us. ☺

Key word:
Immense: extremely large
Synonyms: boundless, colossal, elephantine, endless, enormous

Explanation:
Go with me here and think of the many times God had every right to hit us with that proverbial 2x4. The amazing thing is His amazing grace because He chooses not to.

Prayer:
Thank you, thank you, thank you, Lord, for Your amazing grace. Amen

Day 97

Text:
Dd Today: Nahum 1 The Lord is good, a stronghold in the day of trouble, & He knows those who trust in Him. He knows us, how well do we know Him? ☺

Key word:
Know: be acquainted with as by sight, experience, or report
Synonyms: comprehend, understand

Explanation:
I have made a habit over the 35 years I have served Him to set aside time each day to cultivate a relationship with Him. There is sooooo much to know, but you know, He is my friend.

Prayer:
Again, open our eyes and ears to see You as You really are and to listen as we would to our best friend, for after all, that's who You are. Amen

Day 98

Text:
Dd Today: Pr 26 Where there is no wood, the fire goes out & where there is no gossip, strife ceases. We must watch with our mouth & our ears. 😊

Key word:
Out: to a point or state of extinction, nonexistence
Synonyms: at an end, dead, doused, expired, extinguished

Explanation:
Have you ever been in a conversation and began to listen to what you were saying, suddenly cringed at the thought of what you just said? Exactly!!

Prayer:
As I listen, Lord, make me aware of my words so as to not say anything that would kindle or fan an inflamed situation. Amen

Day 99

Text:
Dd Today: Hab 2:4 lit. The righteous person in or by his faithfulness (firmness, consistency, belief, faith, steadfastness) shall live! How's our faith? 😊

Key word:
Faithfulness: strict or thorough in the performance of duty
Synonyms: steadfastness, consistency, adherence

Explanation:
It is often our lack of consistency that brings about a feeling of self condemnation, which is very difficult to shake. Thank God, He is never the source of such feelings and is our ultimate source of encouragement.

Prayer:
Even though I may lack some consistency, pour out Your love into my every thought and feeling so as to bring me to a true realization of who You are. Amen

Day 100

Text:
Dd Today: Pr 28 says he who tills his land will have plenty of bread. Let's allow the Lord to till our hearts & we will reap the bread of life. 😊

Key word:
Till: to labor, as by plowing or harrowing, upon (land) for the raising of crops; cultivate
Synonyms: cultivate, grow, culture

Explanation:
There have been so many times that after I have gone through a particular circumstance did I realize the tilling that was taking place.

Prayer:
Dig us deep, Lord, and plant your word in the depths or our hearts. Amen

Day 101

Text:
Dd Today: Pr 30 Every word of God is pure; He is a shield to those who put their trust in Him. How's your word life? Who do we trust in? 😊

Key word:
Pure: clean, spotless, or unsullied
Synonyms: undefiled, untarnished, immaculate

Explanation:
I have made every effort to read the Word every day for the last 30 years, and I still have times when I exhaust me before I let Him.

Prayer:
May we always be so in with You that we find ourselves cheering us on from the sidelines. Amen

Day 102

Text:
Dd Today: Acts 21-26 Paul holds firm to his faith against the religious folk even to his own demise in requesting Caesar's judgment. How would you do? 😊

Key word:
Firm: steadfast or unwavering
Synonyms: determined, immovable, staunch, immovable

Explanation:
I remember one time after I had just delivered a message to our newly founded, fledgling church, Linda came up to me and said I don't know where or when you got so religious. She was referring to much of the terminology I had used during the message. If you remember my introduction, I got saved when I was 24, so religion was about as far from me as it could get. Religion can creep in any time.

Prayer:
Lord, may we be naturally spiritual and spiritually natural all the time. Amen

Day 103

Text:
Dd Today: Zech 4 To those rebldg the temple, it is not by might nor by power, but by My Spirit, says the Lord. Wow, sooo true!! Lord, I let go!! 😊

Key word:
let go: to free; release, to become unrestrained; abandon inhibitions
Synonyms: release, abandon, free, discard

Explanation:
There are so many times I look back on my athletic days, when I got to certain point in a game where I was so spent that I felt like I couldn't go another step. Then I would step into the next level we use to call it a second wind. That is when I realized that it was no longer me performing; I had to abandon all reasoning and simply let go.

Prayer:
Lord, transport us to that level where we are no longer dependent on ourselves but totally dependent on You. Amen

Day 104

Text:
Dd Today: Rom 1 God's attributes are clearly seen in His creation, understood by all things, His power Godhead, they are w/out excuse! W/out Excuse, WOW! ☺

Key word:
Excuse: a plea offered in extenuation of a fault or for release from an obligation, promise
Synonyms: justification, pretense, evasion, makeshift

Explanation:
How many times have I, you, or someone else made excuses as to why we couldn't do something, be somewhere, when we really wanted to do almost anything else. Well, there is no excuse to ignore God.

Prayer:
Every time we see the sun, moon or stars, watch it rain or look at cloud formations, see a flower in bloom or fruit on a tree, remind us of where they came from. Amen

Day 105

Text:
Dd Today: Pr 3 Let your heart keep my commands, for length of days, long life & peace they will add to you. I'm all for living a long & peaceful life. ☺

Key word:
Add: to unite or join so as to increase the number, quantity, size, or importance

Synonyms: affix, append, attach, adjoin

Explanation:
When I was in High School in 1970, thinking about the year 2010, 40 years ahead was inconceivable, yet here we are with many more years yet to come. 34 of those years have been with the Lord, and I can safely say that they have not been without their ups and downs, but one thing they haven't lacked is peace.

Prayer:
Put into perspective those things that have been, that are, and that will be, and let peace prevail. Amen

Day 106

Text:
Dd Today: Pr 3 Trust in the Lord w/all your heart & lean not on your own understanding, in all your ways acknowledge Him & He shall direct your paths. Lean on! ☺

Key word:
Lean: to depend or rely
Synonyms: tend, tilt, inclination toward

Explanation:
I remember a time when my wife and I were having some heated fellowship, and she decided to remove herself from the situation by getting out of our car. Now, I could have made her stay in the car, physically I was strong enough; however, when she asked me why I didn't restrain her, I simply replied that I wanted her to have more faith in me than that and trust me. The Lord is the same way; He could over power us but totally wants us to trust Him.

Prayer:
In all that we do, help us to recognize that it is trust that will see us through, not our strength Lord, but Yours. Amen

Day 107

Text:
Dd Today: Pr 4 Keep (guard, put watchman around) your heart w/all diligence, for out of it spring the issues of life. Let's give the gift of life. ☺

Key word:
Spring: to proceed or originate from a specific source or cause
Synonyms: emerge, emanate, issue, flow

Explanation:
So many times I find myself in a position of self talk, most often when something doesn't go quite right and I begin talking to myself, usually out loud. I can instantly tell if my heart is shielded or in the instances I'm thinking of, not so shielded. Pay attention to your thought patterns, for they'll take you places you never dreamed of.

Prayer:
Set up a guard or perimeter around our hearts and minds and keep us focused on Your purposes. Amen

Day 108

Text:
Dd Today: Mal 1 addresses Israel's lack of love for God by bringing imperfect sacrifices, lame, blind & sick. Let's bring our best to Him & see His best. ☺

Key word:
Best: a person's most agreeable or desirable emotional state

Synonyms: pure, moral, conscientious, meritorious, worthy, exemplary, upright

Explanation:
I can't tell you how many times I have gone into a service, and the worship leader asks us all to lift up our hands and my first thought is that I don't FEEL like lifting my hands, but when I yield and begin to give up my pride and the moment I lift those hands, His presence floods me. Every time!!

Prayer:
There is no place like being in Your presence, yielding to You and feeling Your arms wrapped around me. Thank You for Your faithfulness even when I'm not. Amen

Day 109

Text:
Dd Today: Rom 8 Thru Him we received the spirit of adoption, becoming His children even joint heirs w/Christ. God loved us enough to adopt us, Praise the Lord. 😊

Key word:
Adopt: to choose or take as one's own
Synonyms: choose, approve, embrace, take in

Explanation:
Although I have never adopted a child, it is common knowledge that when taken in, an orphan will often display very different behavior traits from when he or she was in the orphanage. It has a calming effect, knowing they are loved from a more permanent perspective.

Prayer:
Lord, open our understanding to see Your love from Your perspective. Amen

Day 110

Text:
Dd Today: Rom 8 What then shall we say to these things? If God be for us, who can be against us? I reiterate, Who can be against us? ☺

Key word:
For: in favor of; on the side of
Synonyms: in favor of, in order to, beneficial to

Explanation:
There are some things that simply cannot be explained away. It is the sovereignty of God that makes it happen, and only because He is for us, can that sovereignty come into play.

Prayer:
Your will be done not ours, Lord. Amen

Day 111

Text:
Dd Today: Rom 8 Who shall separate us from the love of God, tribulation, persecution, famine, peril, sword? Yet in all these things we are more than conquerors. Amen! ☺

Key word:
Separate: to remove or sever from association, service
Synonyms: rupture, sever, demobilize close off

Explanation:
Many years ago when I was in college, some friends of mine and I decided to go to an X rated movie. They showed things in there that should never be seen anywhere, let alone on screen. A few years later I got saved, and I realized at that point that God loves us enough that He'll find His way through all the junk in order to bring us into a relationship with Him.

Prayer:
Thank you, Lord, for loving me enough to come and get me out of the pit, putting me in a place of honor in Your kingdom. Amen

Day 112

Text:
Dd Today: Mal 3 He comes as a refiner's fire & launderer's soap to purge us as gold & silver. Lather me up & turn up the heat Lord, that I may be clean. ☺

Key word:
Purge: to rid of whatever is impure or undesirable; cleanse; purify
Synonyms: cleaning, remove, expel, clarification eradication

Explanation:
There are so many times and circumstances that He has used to sand down my edges and give me a better understanding of how to use the wisdom that is available to me on a daily basis. The refining process isn't always easy but ever so necessary.

Prayer:
Please continue the refining process and make us into a vessel that truly can be used. Amen

Day 113

Text:
Dd Today: Mal 3 tells us not to rob God, but to give & we will not only avoid the curse, we will be blessed so that there will not be room enough for it. Receive it! ☺

Key Word:
Avoid: to prevent from happening
Synonyms: elude, avoid, escape

Explanation:
We haven't always thought we should tithe over the years, and it is those times that didn't, that we experienced the most financial difficulty. We couldn't afford not to give.

Prayer:
We will give to You whatever it is that You ask of us, for it's all Yours anyway. Amen

Day 114

Text:
Dd Today: Mal 4 You who fear My name the Sun of Righteousness shall arise w/healing in His wings & you shall go out & grow fat like stall fed calves. Amen! ☺

Key Word:
Fear: to have reverential awe of
Synonyms: consternation, care, concern

Explanation:
There is something healthy about having a fear of the Lord in us. Without it, we definitely "dwell carelessly" as the Bible says. That fear keeps us on the path knowing that there are consequences for our actions bringing in personal responsibility.

Prayer:
It is a healthy thing to fear Your name; keep us mindful of Your gentle prodding and leading. Amen

Day 115

Text:
Dd Today: Rom 12 We are to present our bodies a living sacrifice...just remember when the heat's turned up, don't jump off the altar. ☺

Key Word:
Present: to bring, offer, or give, often in a formal or ceremonious way
Synonyms: bestow, donate, proffer, yield

Explanation:
Just remember, when you pray and ask the Lord to help you in any given area, He will give you as many opportunities as it takes until you stay on the altar long enough for the sacrifice to be completed. In other words, He'll let you until you'll let Him affect the necessary changes.

Prayer:
We give You free reign in our lives to work in us Your character, allowing us to remain on the altar long enough to be sacrificially successful. Amen

Day 116

Text:
Dd Today: Rom 12 We are not to be conformed to this world, but be transformed renewing your mind, that we may prove the good & acceptable perfect will of God. ☺

Key Word:
Transformed: to undergo a change in form, appearance, or character
Synonyms: mutate, reconstruct, translate, alter, transfigure

Explanation:
How many times have I caught myself in a thought pattern that I know is absolutely wrong, taking me down a path that will eventually alter my behavior in a negative way? For example, when your wife gives you advice and you know it's right, but your pride gets in the way and off you go on one of those unfruitful bunny trails.

Prayer:
Apprehend us in our thoughts, so as to transform our thinking. Amen

Day 117

Text:
Dd Today: Gen 1 In the beginning God, stop! Isn't that enough!! Praise the Lord! ☺

Key Word:
Beginning: the point of time or space at which anything begins
Synonyms: initiation, inauguration, inception

Explanation:
The thing we all have to remember is that He started it all and He will finish it.

Prayer:
Thank You Lord, for creating us in the first place and saving us from ourselves. Amen

Day 118

Text:
Dd Today: Gen 3 They heard the sound of the Lord God walking in the garden. Even after their eyes had been opened, it didn't impair their hearing. Shh listen. ☺

Key Word:
Heard: to be capable of perceiving sound by the ear; have the faculty of perceiving sound vibrations
Synonyms: attend, regard, listen

Explanation:
When you set aside time to be with the Lord, always remember to take the time to listen for Him and to Him. He'll be faithful to speak if we'll stop ours.

Prayer:
We are so grateful that You are a God who longs to communicate with us. Would You open our ears and shut our mouth long enough to hear what You have to say? Amen

Day 119

Text:
Dd Today: Gen 6 Noah found grace in the eyes of the Lord, he was a just man, perfect in his generations. Oh that we would be found like Noah in the eyes of the Lord. ☺

Key Word:
Found: to locate, attain, or obtain by search or effort
Synonyms: achieve, win, earn, acquire

Explanation:
The Lord searched to and fro on the face of the earth to find a man who would stand in the gap for His purposes. Noah was such a man, what about us?

Prayer:
Lord, look upon us with the favor You gave Noah as we stand in the gap for our families and our generation. Amen

Day 120

Text:
Dd Today: Gen 8 The Ark rested & Noah waited 2 wks until he heard God spk to confirm their departure from the Arc. God will spk in His time to guide us. ☺

Key Word:
Confirm: to make firm or more firm; add strength to; settle or establish firmly
Synonyms: affirm, bear out, endorse, thumbs up, validate

Explanation:
God is never lacking when it comes to specific guidance and direction for our lives. I can remember Him speaking out loud to me four times because it was the only way He could get my attention at the time to confirm to me what I should do.

Prayer:
Lord, we give You permission to interrupt what we are doing in order to confirm exactly what we are to do in a given circumstance. Amen

Day 121

Text:
Dd Today: Pr 21 When the wise receive instruction, he receives knowledge. If we cease to learn, we cease...... ☺

Key Word:
Instruction: knowledge or information imparted
Synonyms: commandment, order, information, tutoring plan, word

Explanation:
There is a never-ending battle in our minds between lethargy and self motivation. Learning and the process thereof will keep us on the motivated side and not let us lapse into stagnation.

Prayer:
Lord, would You give a swift kick in the pants when we even show signs of becoming apathetic. Thanks, Amen

Day 122

Text:
Dd Today: 1 Cor 10 Let him who thinks he stands take heed lest he fall. No temptation has overtaken you except such as is common to man. Are we unique, NOT! 😊

Key Word:
Overtaken: to catch up with and pass, as in a race; move by
Synonyms: overhaul, better, strike, hit, catch up, engulf

Explanation:
We all have the impression that what we are going through is a completely unique circumstance or event and that no one has ever seen it like we have it. As we can see by what Paul said, it simply isn't true. When you think you are going through a rough time, look around; it only takes a few seconds to see there always someone worse off than you.

Prayer:
Lord, lift our vision higher and help us to see others before ourselves. Amen

Day 123

Text:
Dd Today: 2 Ch 10 Rehoboam rejected the advice of the older men & instead asked the opinion of the young men. Wise counsel may not be easy, but it is, wise! 😊

Key Word:
Rejected: To discard as defective or useless; throw away
Synonyms: abandoned, dropped, deserted, forsaken

Explanation:
Advice is great as long as it lines up with what He says, not with what you want to hear.

Prayer:
Never let us reject Your advice no matter what the source, but always confirm it with Your peace and calm. Amen

Day 124

Text:
Dd Today: Gen 14,15 Abram refused any of the spoil, gave a tithe to Melchizedek. God said, don't be afraid, I am your great reward. He believed God, do we? 😊

Key Word:
Refused: to decline to accept
Synonyms: vetoed, prohibited, rejected

Explanation:
Abram knew if he honored the One who gave all to him in the first place that He would honor him in return. Seek ye first the kingdom of God, and all these things will be added to you. Put Him first.

Prayer:
From this time forward help us to always put You first, whether it be finances or what we say or what we do. Amen

Day 125

Text:
Dd Today: 1 Cor 12 God has set the members, many, yet 1 body. We are His body, members individually, uniquely gifted, qualified. Rise up, go forth, function. 😊

Key Word:
Qualified: having the qualities, accomplishments, etc., that fit a person for some function, office, or the like
Synonyms: competent, equivocal, worthy, fitted, proper

Explanation:
I can remember the first time I gave a word to a group of people. It was a home group, and as I was praying the night before our meeting, the Lord gave me a word for every single person. I was totally shocked, but believe me He wasn't. We all have gifts and need to exercise them.

Prayer:
Lord, make clear to us our gifts and qualifications as we are faithful to step out. Amen

Day 126

Text:
Dd Today: 1 Cor 13 When I was a child, I spoke, understood & thought as a child, but when I became a man, I put away childish things. Be like them not as them. ☺

Key Word:
Childish: Marked by or indicating a lack of maturity

Synonyms: infantine, kid stuff, adolescent, unsophisticated, immature

Explanation:
Paul is very clear that he wants us to grow-up in our faith. We are to act appropriately, not as children but as adults. His qualification is that we don't lose our childlike innocence in our approach to our heavenly Father.

Prayer:
As opportunities come to respond to Your love, we commit our response to be that of child to a true loving Father. Amen

Day 127

Text:
Dd Today: Pr 25 Though the wicked may attack our dwelling & seem to have the upper hand. Yet a righteous man may fall 7 times, he will get up again! Get up! ☺

Key Word:
Get up: to sit up or stand; arise
Synonyms: stand, rise and shine, awaken

Explanation:
Our biggest successes usually come out of a series of mistakes, Get up!!

Prayer:
Illuminate our understanding of our mistakes and help us to turn them into a series of opportunities. Amen

Day 128

Text:
Dd Today: 1 Cor 15 Paul exhorts us, do not be deceived; evil company corrupts good habits. Hangin out? Who with? ☺

Key Word:
Corrupts: to destroy or subvert the honesty or integrity of
Synonyms: undermine, bestialize, waste debauched, deprave, pollute

Explanation:
We've been told this for years. You become like the people you hang around with not the other way around.

Prayer:
Would You lead us to the relationships which will strengthen us first, then those that we can strengthen? Amen

Day 129

Text:
Dd Today: Gen 21 The Lord visited Sarah as He had said, the Lord did for Sarah as He had spoken. The Lord always does what He says. He never disappoints. ☺

Key Word:
Always: every time; on every occasion; without exception
Synonyms: evermore, till hell freezes over, constantly, invariably

Explanation:
The one thing we can count on with the Lord is that we can always count on the Lord. No matter what the circumstance, event or condition, He will never leave us or forsake us.

Prayer:
Thank You, Lord, that we can depend on You even though we often fall short on our end. Amen

Day 130

Text:
Dd Today: Gen 22 Abraham w/held nothing from the Lord, even his only son. God blessed him beyond measure. Let's w/hold nothing from Him & see his blessing. ☺

Key Word:
Withhold: to refrain from giving or granting
Synonyms: disallow, sit on, abstain, refrain, hold out

Explanation:
In the fullest sense of the word, Abraham took what was most valuable to him, God's promised his son and was willing to go through with the sacrifice. In our humanity, I'm not so sure I could do what Abraham so ably accomplished. However, that being said, where are we putting our trust?

Prayer:
There is a level of trust, Lord, that only comes through obedience to Your word, knowing that You, above all, have our best interests at heart. Amen

Day 131

Text:
Dd Today: 2 Cor 3 The people could not look at Moses w/out the veil, but in Christ the veil is removed & we are transformed in His image glory to glory. Unveiled! ☺

Key Word:
Look: to turn one's eyes toward something or in some direction in order to see
Synonyms: watch, gaze, glance

Explanation:
Have you ever lead someone to the Lord and afterwards their face or countenance is completely different? It is the same type of encounter that Moses had before he came down the mountain. When we meet the Lord, we are changed.

Prayer:
When we meet with You, pour out on us Your transforming power so that even our facial appearance is very different. Amen

Day 132

Text:
Dd Today: Pr 2 If you receive, treasure, incline, apply, cry out, seek & search for wisdom, understanding. Then you will find the fear & knowledge of the Lord. AAAmen!! ☺

Key Word:
Search: to look at or examine (a person, object, etc.) carefully in order to find something concealed
Synonyms: research, explore, look over, hunt

Explanation:
There is no greater attribute of the Lord that we could seek for than wisdom. Solomon understood this, and it was the only thing he asked God for even when God Himself asked him what he wanted.

Prayer:
Grant us wisdom above all else, Lord, for ourselves and for all our family members. Amen

Day 133

Text:
Dd Today: Pr 3 Do not forget My law, keep My commands; for length of days, long life & peace they will add to you. Living long & peace, yesss, don't forget? ☺

Key Word:
Keep: to conform to; follow; fulfill
Synonyms: reserve, retain, withhold, preserve

Explanation:
There is a promise contained in this verse which basically guarantees our longevity and contentment. It is in reading the Word, but not only in reading, but also in applying it directly to our daily lives, working it out if you will.

Prayer:
Father, open Your word to us in a new dimension, so that we are able to not only comprehend it, but also realize its applicable nature. Amen

Day 134

Text:
Dd Today: Pr 4 Wisdom is the principle thing, therefore get wisdom. And in all you getting, get understanding. Loving wisdom & understanding makes us secure. 😊

Key Word:
Secure: free from care; without anxiety
Synonyms: protected, safe, stable, fast, fixed, confident

Explanation:
There is a freedom that comes with knowing deep down in your knower that you know.

Prayer:
We confidently come before You, knowing that You know and consequently we will know. Amen

Day 135

Text:
Dd Today: 2 Cor 10 The weapons of our warfare are not carnal but mighty in God for the pulling down of strongholds. Let's build up our spiritual arsenal! 😊

Key Word:
Mighty: having, characterized by, or showing superior power or strength
Synonyms: omnipotent, potent, indomitable

Explanation:
There is a certain amount of our walk with God that requires us to depend on Him. Yeah, like ALL of it!!!

Prayer:
We all know we are supposed to depend on you in everything that we do; would You show us tangibly how this works? Amen

Day 136

Text:
Dd Today: 2 Cor 10 We are not to compare ourselves among ourselves, for not he who commends himself is approved, but whom the Lord commends. Let's see as He sees. ☺

Key Word:
Compare: to examine (two or more objects, ideas, people, etc.) in order to note similarities and differences
Synonyms: contrast, resemble, vie, identify with

Explanation:
The key here is to realize that He made us all unique, and in that uniqueness, there is no one else on the planet that has the same qualities we do. So comparing ourselves will only bring frustration.

Prayer:
Guide us in seeing ourselves as the unique individuals You see us as. Amen

Day 137

Text:
Dd Today: 2 Cor 12 My grace is sufficient for you, My strength is made perfect in weakness. For when we are weak, then we are strong. We need You, Lord!! ☺

Key Word:
Sufficient: adequate for the purpose; enough
Synonyms: adequate, ample, proportionate, enough

Explanation:
We all have a great deal of trouble understanding that our weakness has everything to do with how strong we really are. He has no weaknesses, and therefore will jump in when we need it the most and make up for our inadequacies.

Prayer:
There is a place where we find ourselves in You. It is in our weaknesses. Would You bring us to an understanding of what our weaknesses are and then most of all allow You to fill those gaps for us? Amen

Day 138

Text:
Dd Today: Gen 32 Jacob wrestled with God and prevailed. He was desperate for fear of his brother yet rewarded for his tenacity. Let's be tenacious with God. 😊

Key Word:
Tenacious: pertinacious, persistent, stubborn, or obstinate
Synonyms: stiff-necked, sturdy, steadfast, firm

Explanation:
God is the perfect Father and simply will not just give us something because we want it. He gives what we need and through the process wants us to be tenacious with our desires. Enough so that He cannot ignore us.

Prayer:
Lord, would you help us to realize You're not just a microwave up there in the sky, popping out instant gratification. Amen

Day 139

Text:
Dd Today: 2 Cor 13 Paul prayed that we may be made complete (making the necessary repairs as in mending nets, equipping). In what state are your nets? ☺

Key Word:
Complete: having all parts or elements; lacking nothing; whole; entire; full
Synonyms: entire, intact, perfect

Explanation:
The Disciples, being fisherman, understood that if their nets were in disrepair they would have a hard time catching and keeping any fish. The same is true of the nets we throw out to fish for men. If we are not prepared for the catch, discipling, teaching, grooming, etc. we will have a hard time keeping them.

Prayer:
Lord, would You heal our short sightedness and keep us mindful of what it take to not only catch the fish, but keep the catch. Amen

Day 140

Text:
Dd Today: Gal 2 Paul encourages us in a day of compromise, not to compromise in our Faith, but to be strong, holding to the truth. Let's stand & be counted. ☺

Key Word:
Compromise: to expose or make vulnerable to danger, suspicion, scandal, etc.; jeopardize
Synonyms: give in, settlement, sell out, settle, endanger, jeopardize

Explanation:
How many times have we been in a situation where we settled for less than what it was we wanted out of the deal, i.e. paid more than we needed to? Paul is telling us not to settle for less than the best. There is the best, then there's all the rest.

Prayer:
Well up within us, Lord, so that we resist the temptation to settle for less than Your best. Amen

Day 141

Text:
Dd Today: Gal 4 Paul says we have been adopted by the Lord, therefore we are sons & by virtue of that fact, heirs of God thru Christ. YOU'RE A KING'S KID!! ☺

Key Word:
Adopted: to take and rear (the child of other parents) as one's own child, specifically by a formal legal act
Synonyms: affirm, take in, take up, ratify, choose, opt

Explanation:
We must understand and come to the realization that when we got saved, the Lord formally brought us into His family and legally made us equal heirs along with His Son.

Prayer:
Thank You Lord for taking us into Your family and adopting us Your own. Amen

Day 142

Text:
Dd Today: Gen 37 Joseph, though accused by his brothers, kept his dream alive in his heart. Feed your dreams for they will grow & one day bare fruit. ☺

Key Word:
Dream: an aspiration; goal; aim
Synonyms: vision, conceive

Explanation:
Dreams are like a plant, if left without water, they will wither and die. In Joseph's case, he spent over a decade in and out of prison, weathering accusations and finally realizing his dreams, which only benefited his family.

Prayer:
As we water our dreams, show us the direction we should go which will take us where our dreams become reality. Amen

Day 143

Text:
Dd Today: Gal 5 The fruit of the Spirit is love, joy, peace, longsuffering, kindness, goodness, faithfulness, gentleness, self-control. Fruits R US!! ☺

Key Word:
Fruit: anything produced or accruing; product, result, or effect
Synonyms: reward, produce, harvest product

Explanation:
When we look at the fruits of the Spirit, they always are associated with an outward manifestation of an inward experience having to do with the infilling of the H.S. The Bible Dictionary says fruits are those gracious dispositions and habits which the Spirit produces in those in whom he dwells and works.

Prayer:
Fill us again and again and again with Your Holy Spirit so that the fruits thereof might be seen and experienced by those we touch. Amen

Day 144

Text:
Dd Today: Gal 6 Let us not grow weary while doing good, in due season we shall reap if we don't lose heart. Sowing good is always the right thing. 😊

Key Word:
Reap: to get as a return, recompense, or result
Synonyms: retrieve, garner, profit, pick, realize

Explanation:
Has there ever been a time when you did something good for someone, helped a neighbor, visited someone in the hospital, paid someone else's bill, etc. and felt bad about it?

Prayer:
Let the realization of doing something good sink in, so that we never cease to serve. Amen

Day 145

Text:
Dd Today: Eph 3 To know the love of Christ which passes knowledge, that we may be filled w/all the fullness of God. Let's participate in ALL He has for us. 😊

Key Word:
All: the whole of (used in referring to quantity, extent, or duration)
Synonyms: complete, everything, sum total, outright

Explanation:
I can remember many times being in church services over the years and experiencing what felt like a cloud enveloping the room causing various responses from different individuals: crying, kneeling, laying, dancing, etc. We were totally immersed in His presence. This was in a corporate gathering, but I have

also experienced His presence by giving a word of knowledge or wisdom, preaching, teaching, counseling and so on. Let Him and He will.

Prayer:
Keep us from putting You in a box and limiting Your ability to function through our lives. Amen

Day 146

Text:
Dd Today: Pr 16 Commit your works to the Lord and you thoughts will be established. Committing is like lifting a load off your mind. ☺

Key Word:
Commit: to bind or obligate, as by pledge or assurance
Synonyms: carry out, effect, execute

Explanation:
In a world where the word commit is treated like a disease, we Christians find solace in the term because not only did we commit our lives to Him, but in return He makes a commitment to never leave us or forsake us. I know my wife loves to hear a yes or a no, a commitment one way or the other, none of this wishy-washy stuff.

Prayer:
Lord, let our yes be yes and our no be no. Amen

Day 147

Text:
Dd Today: Eph 4 Put off you former conduct, the old man, be renewed in the spirit of your mind, in true righteousness & holiness. No sub for thinking right. ☺

Key Word:
Renewed: to restore or replenish; to revive; reestablish
Synonyms: Restored, recovered, revived, improved

Explanation:
There are so many times I can think of in which my mind went off, and most of them had to do with some correction or input my wife gave me. I knew she was correct, and I just couldn't accept the fact. This is where stinking thinking can absolutely destroy any kind of communication. We have to get control over our heads.

Prayer:
Work in us, Lord, the art of self control, especially in the area of our minds. Amen

Day 148

Text:
Dd Today: Eph 4 Be angry & do not sin: don't let the sun go down on your wrath, nor give an opportunity to the devil. Always make it right, feelings or no. ☺

Key Word:
Always: every time; on every occasion; without exception
Synonyms: invariably, evermore, till hell freezes over, ever

Explanation:
We have had many occasions to stay up late at night talking through a disagreement, committing before hand to seeing it through to a conclusion. I must admit that 99%, if not all, of them were my lack of response.

Prayer:
Lord, help us to see the value in working through our differences and never waking up in the morning with unresolved issues. Amen

Day 149

Text:
Dd Today: Eph 4 Let no corrupt word proceed out of your mouth, but let your words always edify & be as a gift to the hearer. Nuff said!! ☺

Key Word:
Gift: something given voluntarily without payment in return, as to show favor toward someone, honor an occasion, or make a gesture of assistance; present
Synonyms: donation, contribution, offering, endowment, gratuity

Explanation:
There are plenty of opportunities each day to let our mouths simply run off without the slightest thought to how it will affect the one who has to hear whatever it was we ran off about. We must take thought before we speak in order to present our listeners with presents to their ears instead of needing muffs.

Prayer:
Let the words of our mouth and meditations of our heart be acceptable in Your sight and the ears of others, oh Lord. Amen

Day 150

Text:
Dd Today: Eph 6 Take up the whole armor of God, that you may be able to w/stand in the evil day. Having done all, to STAND! Don't give him an inch. ☺

Key Word:
Whole: comprising the full quantity, amount, extent, number, etc., without diminution or exception
Synonyms: undiminished, integral, complete

Explanation:
As one old scholar put it, **"I have so much to do that I shall spend the first three hours in prayer."** — Martin Luther We need His protection each and every day; however, if we only put on a portion of His allotted armor, then we will only get a portion of His allotted protection.

Prayer:
May we never approach a day out from under the protection of Your wings. Amen

Day 151

Text:
Dd Today: Phil 1 Be confident of this very thing, that He who has begun a good work in you will complete it. So let go and let Him do it! ☺

Key Word:
Complete: to make whole or entire, to bring to an end; finish
Synonyms: finish, close, conclude

Explanation:
He is never one who will leave a job undone and is definitely committed to seeing us through to the end of our finishing school.

Prayer:
There is much emphasis on letting go these days, but help us to not only let go, but let You have free reign in our lives to do what must be done. Amen

Day 152

Text:
Dd Today: Phil 2 It is God who works in you both to will and to do for His good pleasure. Remember it is for HIS good pleasure & ours will be realized. ☺

Key Word:
Will: the act or process of using or asserting one's choice
Synonyms: choice, pleasure, inclination, resolution, decision

Explanation:
It is only through the submission of our will that His will be accomplished.

Prayer:
Not ours, but Yours will be done. Amen

Day 153

Text:
Dd Today: Pr 22 Do not remove the ancient boundaries, which your fathers have set. Make sure the spiritual foundation in your life is sure. Sure, you *will* be. ☺

Key Word:
Remove: to get rid of; do away with; put an end to
Synonyms: take, cut out, erase, eliminate, obliterate, uproot

Explanation:
There are many moments in our lives that we can look back to, which changed the course or modified the direction we were on, and it is those markers we are not to forget, but look back to and remember just what it was that caused us to make the change.

Prayer:
Lord, we appreciate every time You put some event or person or experience in our life that caused us to see the path we were on and move on toward changing that direction. Amen

Day 154

Text:
Dd Today: Phil 4 Be anxious for nothing, in everything by prayer & supplication, w/thanksgiving, let your requests be made known to God. Result=Peace!! ☺

Key Word:
Everything: All things or all of a group of things
Synonyms: sum, totality, universe, whole caboodle, all

Explanation:
It is when we hold back nothing that everything comes into focus.

Prayer:
Lord, all that I have, all that I am, all that I ever will be is Yours. Amen

Day 155

Text:
Dd Today: Col 2 We were dead in our sin, but Christ has forgiven our sin, has Wiped out the very record against us, both Principalities & Powers. A clean slate! ☺

Key Word:
Forgiven: to grant pardon for or remission of (an offense, debt, etc.); absolve, in spite of your feelings
Synonyms: reinstated, pardoned

Exlanation:
Sin is the element that separates us and causes us to hide from God. Forgiveness is the force that heals that sin-created gap and brings us back into right standing with God.

Prayer:
Please forgive us and give us the strength to release forgiveness to all who have wronged us in any way. Amen

Day 156

Text:
Dd Today: Ex 1 Though Pharaoh made the Israelites labor harder, yet they multiplied all the more. When the pressure is on what comes out of you? ☺

Key Word:
Pressure: a constraining or compelling force or influence
Synonyms: distress, trouble, impel, tension, press

Explanation:
Can you think of any situations where you cowed to peer pressure or simply went along with the crowd? We've all had opportunities to react or respond to pressure, what is it in your life? Respond, don't react.

Prayer:
When given the opportunity to stand, Lord, give us the strength and conviction to do so. Amen

Day 157

Text:
Dd Today: Phil 4 Whatever things are true, noble, just, pure, lovely, of good report, if there is anything praiseworthy, meditate on these things. What were you thinking? ☺

Key Word:
Praiseworthy: deserving of praise; laudable
Synonyms: deserving, honorable, reputable

Explanation:
What were you thinking after reading all these wonderful words? The first words that came to me were, is that possible? Of course I know it is, and it would do all of us a good service to start our days dwelling on something other than what we tend to dwell on now.

Prayer:
Flood my thoughts and meditations with Phil 4, thank you. Amen

Day 158

Text:
Dd Today: Ex 4 Even Moses was unsure & insecure when God called him, nevertheless he went with it & history was made. When you're unsure & insecure, God isn't! ☺

Key Word:
Insecure: subject to fears, doubts, etc.; not self-confident or assured; not confident or certain; uneasy; anxious
Synonyms: unprotected, unstable, rickety, uptight, unsafe, unsound

Explanation:
God took Moses and turned him into someone many put above everyone else and sometimes even equated him with God Himself, yet Moses, Abraham, Isaac, Jacob, Peter, James, John, Paul were all men just like you and me.

Prayer:
Help us in our frailness to accept who we are and move on into who You want us to be. Amen

Day 159

Text:
Dd Today: Pr 28 He who covers his sins will not prosper, but whoever confesses & forsakes them will have mercy. Being an open book, gives Him the pen. ☺

Key Word:
Covers: to hide from view; screen
Synonyms: cloak, conceal, hide, screen

Explanation:
Have you ever noticed that no matter how hard we work to conceal a matter, it always comes around to bite us in the end? It's always better to be truthful; the consequences aren't nearly as terrible as they seemed at the time.

Prayer:
Put a holy conviction in our heart to always be truthful, regardless of the circumstances. Amen

Day 160

Text:
Dd Today: Ex 5 Pharaoh hardened his heart. He, who is often rebuked & hardens his neck, will suddenly be destroyed w/out remedy. Hard or soft, our choice! ☺

Key Word:
Destroyed: to reduce (an object) to useless fragments, a useless form, or remains, as by rending, burning, or dissolving; injure beyond repair or renewal; demolish; ruin; annihilate
Synonyms: smashed, broken, wrecked, blasted, wasted, ruined, obliterated

Explanation:
Nobody wants to be destroyed, really. But each time we harden our hearts, become defensive, prideful, and arrogant we are taking a very big step toward destruction.

Prayer:
As Ezekial put it, remove from me a heart of stone and replace it with a heart of flesh. Amen

Day 161

Text:
Dd Today: 1 Thes 5 Rejoice Always, pray w/out ceasing, in Everything give thanks; for this is THE will of God in Christ Jesus for You. The Will of God? For me? ☺

Key Word:
Always: every time; on every occasion; without exception
Synonyms: perpetually, everlastingly, continuously

Explanation:
Sometimes when reading the Word, we somehow come to the conclusion that the particular verse is for someone else, but God is trying to get through to us, that's all. He wants us to apply the verse to our daily living, rejoice always, pray without ceasing, in everything give thanks. For us!

Prayer:
In all that we do, let it be unto You. Amen

Day 162

Text:
Dd Today: Pr 3 Do not forget my law, let your heart keep my commands, for length of days, long life & peace they will add to you. Suggestion? I think not! ☺

Key Word:
Forget: to cease or fail to remember; be unable to recall
Synonyms: overlook, disregard, disremember, ignore

Explanation:
There are no suggestions in scripture, and this is not the one exception. I think we could all use a little more life and peace, don't you?

Prayer:
Help us to be like David in that we meditate on Your law day and night. Amen

Day 163

Text:
Dd Today: Pr 4 Keep your heart with all diligence, for out it spring the issues of life. Garbage in, garbage out, let's put our spam filters on high. ☺

Key Word:
Issues: the act of sending out or putting forth; promulgation; distribution
Synonyms: flow, emanate, arise, spring

Explanation:
In our world of technology, we all understand that what we feed our computing devices will produce an answer based on that information, no more no less. Bad information, bad answers, good information, good answers. In kind, what we feed ourselves will determine the quality or lack thereof of our lives.

Prayer:
Remind us daily, Lord, to protect or guard our heart, knowing that what we let in surely will come out. Amen

Day 164

Text:
Dd Today: Ex 10 Darkness fell for 3 days in Egypt, but the Israelites had light in their dwellings. Darkness may close in around us, but we have the Light. ☺

Key Word:
Light: the radiance or illumination from a particular source
Synonyms: illumine, radiate

Explanation:
Whenever we see someone come to the Lord, they very often take on a new radiance or glow about them. This is the inner illumination of the Spirit of the living God. The very same Spirit that raised Christ from the dead lives within us and can't help but shine through us if we will let Him.

Prayer:
Let Your light shine through us, oh Lord, as we live out our everyday lives. Amen

Day 165

Text:
Dd Today: 1 Tim 1 This charge I commit to you, according to the prophecies previously made concerning you, by them wage good warfare. Place to start? Knees? ☺

Key Word:
Warfare: armed conflict between two massed enemies, armies, or the like
Synonyms: contention, hostility, strife

Explanation:
If you have ever received a prophetic word, Paul says to wage good warfare with it. He obviously didn't mean to go out and pick a fight, but to get on your knees and assault the heavens to see that word bear fruit in your life.

Prayer:
Come to our aid, Lord, and send your angels to fight alongside us that we might advance against the adversary of our souls and see Your words come to fruition. Amen

Day 166

Text:
Dd Today: Pr 7 Treasure my commands w/in you, write them on the tablet of your heart. What is written on your tablet? His words are a lamp & a light. ☺

Key Word:
Treasure: to regard or treat as precious; cherish
Synonyms: value, esteem

Explanation:
I went to some special meetings one time, back in the early 90's. I answered a call for prayer and when the person who was praying for me touched my forehead, I had an instant vision of my heart as a blackboard and an eraser came and eliminated everything I had previously written on it. Then, the Lord's hand began to write on it His agenda instead of mine. The thought here is to allow Him to erase and rewrite.

Prayer:
Lord, not our agenda be done, but Yours be written on the tablet of our hearts. Amen

Day 167

Text:
Dd Today: Ex 15 Moses sang, 'I will sing to the Lord, for He has triumphed gloriously! The horse & its rider he has thrown into the sea!' Trust God, they did. ☺

Key Word:
Triumphed: to gain a victory; be victorious; win
Synonyms: success, victory, succeed, celebration, jubilation

Explanation:
I think the key here is instead of exhausting our every resource and then turning to God, it's turn to God and let Him exhaust His resources on our behalves, which we know He can never run out of.

Prayer:
Lord, teach us to know when our resources are valuable and above all trust You before ourselves. Amen

Day 168

Text:
Dd Today: Ex 16 Even though the people were given quail & Manna, some were still disobedient, gathered more than they needed & it 'stank'. Let's obey & stink not. ☺

Key Word:
Disobedient: refusal or failure to obey
Synonyms: insubordinate, contumacious, defiant, rebellious, unsubmissive, uncompliant

Explanation:
I find it hard to believe that being supplied food every day and all you had to do was to gather enough for your family and

no more, they still got greedy and wanted more. The human condition never ceases to amaze.

Prayer:
Thank You, Lord, for providing us with what we need and not necessarily what we want. Amen

Day 169

Text:
Dd Today: 2 Tim 1 Paul reminds Timothy to stir up the gift of God, which is in you through the laying on of hands. We have no less calling than to do the same. ☺

Key Word:
Stir up: to rouse from inactivity, quiet, contentment, indifference
Synonyms: rouse, foment, arouse, provoke, stimulate, goad, spur

Explanation:
Before I ever went out to Pastor, I had been challenged to stir up my gifts. The only issue was what were my gifts? The process that followed was very enlightening because all He asked me to do was what I found right in front of me on a daily basis. Talking with those I worked with, praying when the need arose, speaking up and not being silent, the list goes on.

Prayer:
Lord, reveal our gifts is such a way that we can only recognize them for what they really are. Amen

Day 170

Text:
Dd Today: 2 Tim 1 For God has not given us a spirit of fear, but of power & of love & of a SOUND MIND. Safe thinking, good judgment! We have it all, amen? ☺

Key Word:
Sound: free from injury, damage, defect, disease, etc.; in good condition; healthy; robust
Synonyms: unharmed, whole, hale, unbroken, hardy

Explanation:
Paul was very good at reminding us that God is everything to us, including our peace of mind. We must remember that fear is f-alse e-vidence a-ppearing r-eal. Always falling back on what we know to be true; the basic biblical fundamentals of our faith is what will keep us grounded when all else is crumbling.

Prayer:
When we find ourselves in times of trouble, only Jesus comes to us, speaking words of wisdom, let Him be. Amen

Day 171

Text:
Dd Today: Ex 17 Even as Aaron & Hur supported Moses' hands, when we encounter difficult situations, we must support each other. After all He is our Banner. 😊

Key Word:
Support: a person or thing that gives aid or assistance
Synonyms: maintain, sustain, uphold

Explanation:
I remember a time right after Linda and I first got married. I became sick and couldn't get out of bed. Never before had I experienced anything like this, but our friends at the time came, some 10-15 people, and gathered round my bed and prayed. I had been in bed for almost a week with the doctors not knowing what I had, but after their prayer, I was up and back to work the following Monday. This is known as lifting the hands of those who need it so they can prevail in the battle.

Prayer:
Lord, help us to be sensitive to those around us who need their hands lifted. Amen

Day 172

Text:
Dd Today: 2 Tim 2 Nevertheless the solid foundation of God stands, having this seal: the Lord knows those who are His. Always rely on His foundation. ☺

Key Word:
Foundation: the natural or prepared ground or base on which some structure rests
Synonyms: footing, establishment, settlement

Explanation:
There are certain basic fundamentals we need to learn in order to perform well at anything. In sports if you don't have the basics down, you'll find it very difficult to operate in a team environment. Everything becomes unpredictable, but when you have the proper foundation in operation, everyone can relax and enjoy playing the game.

Prayer:
Lord, help us never to forget the landmarks or fundamentals of our faith and to stand. Amen

Day 173

Text:
Dd Today: 2 Tim 2 In a great house there are many vessels, gold, silver, wood, clay, some for honor-useful, & some for dishonor. Is your vessel useful? ☺

Key Word:
Useful: of practical use, as for doing work; producing material results; supplying common needs
Synonyms: profitable, efficacious, beneficial

Explanation:
When I first became a Christian, we went to a very good Bible based church and received excellent teaching. The only problem with sitting under such good teaching is you can get used to sitting under excellent teaching and never get out and use what you have learned. One practice our Pastor encouraged us to do was to get out and to help other churches either on missions or smaller startup churches. In other words, become a useful vessel.

Prayer:
Lord, challenge us out of our complacency to become useful vessels in Your kingdom. Amen

Day 174

Text:
Dd Today: 2 Tim 2 All scripture is given by inspiration of God & is profitable... That we may be complete, thoroughly equipped for every Good Work. Good Work! ☺

Key Word:
Equipped: to furnish with the qualities necessary for performance
Synonyms: outfit, furnish

Explanation:
Sitting under such good teaching early on in my walk with God, I simply took for granted things that I discovered later were the very things that kept me on track when others were faltering. I soon learned never to take anything for granted and made sure, when I became a pastor, to teach my people those very same things.

Prayer:
Lord, never let us take anything for granted regarding our foundations. Amen

Day 175

Text:
Dd Today: Pr 16 The heart of the wise teaches his mouth, & adds learning to his lips. Solomon & Jesus agree, out of the heart a man speaks. Let's speak life! 😊

Key Word:
Teach: to impart knowledge of or skill in; give instruction in
Synonyms: inform, enlighten, discipline, drill, school, indoctrinate

Explanation:
I've heard it so many times through the years that it rings in my ears. We have one mouth and two feet, so we need to walk it twice as much as we talk it. Speak life, it's always possible.

Prayer:
Lord, help us to do more than we say. Amen

Day 176

Text:
Dd Today: Pr 17 A merry heart does good like a medicine... like a disease, go out & infect someone with cheer & a genuine smile. 😊

Key Word:
Merry: full of cheerfulness or gaiety; joyous in disposition or spirit
Synonyms: happy, blithe, frolicsome, cheery, glad

Explanation:
We have so many opportunities each day to make someone's day, and often times all that involves is a genuine smile.

Prayer:
Keep us mindful that bringing cheer to someone else is the best way to bring cheer to ourselves. Amen

Day 177

Text:
Dd Today: Pr 18 The name of the Lord is a strong tower, the righteous run into it & are safe. We may run to many places, but only one is truly safe. ☺

Key Word:
Safe: secure from liability to harm, injury, danger, or risk
Synonyms: protected, sound, guarded, secure

Explanation:
When I played quarterback, I always had some big guys lining up in front of me to protect me, but somehow that never was enough. No matter how big and strong they were, someone always managed to get through, and I'd end up running for my life. But when God forms a pocket, nothing gets through.

Prayer:
Thank You for providing a place that we can go which is truly a sanctuary from the outside world. Amen

Day 178

Text:
Dd Today: Heb 3 Of Israel, many heard God's word, but failed to obey, which deprived them of entering in. Far be it from us that we should be hearers only. ☺

Key Word:
Heard: to perceive (sound) by the ear
Synonyms: attend, hear, listen

Explanation:
So many times Linda will engage me in a conversation right in the middle of a game on the TV. I can hear every word she says, but if you were to ask me to tell you what she said, I would have a terrible time recalling any of it. So it can also be with God's word. We have many distractions that will keep us from really hearing what He wants us to hear.

Prayer:
Lord, would You help us to focus our attention on You and break through all the distractions. Amen

Day 179

Text:
Dd Today: Heb 4 The word of God is living & powerful, sharper than any 2 edged sword, piercing soul, spirit, joints, marrow, even thoughts, intents. Just Read It! ☺

Key Word:
Piercing: to penetrate into or run through (something), as a sharp, pointed dagger, object, or instrument does
Synonyms: enter, puncture, pierce, penetrate

Explanation:
I have read the Word now consistently, virtually every day, for the past 34 plus years, and it never ceases to amaze me at how it can bring clarity to and make sense of any given circumstance I find myself in.

Prayer:
Speak to us, Lord, through Your word by making it fresh every day. Amen

Day 180

Text:
Dd Today: Ex 27 The lamp in the Tabernacle was to be tended so it would burn continually. Our lamp, the HS, needs tending as well. Tending kept the oil fresh? ☺

Key Word:
Fresh: retaining the original properties unimpaired; not stale or spoiled
Synonyms: invigorating, sweet, unadulterated

Explanation:
The priests used to go in and trim, fill, making sure the wicks would burn their brightest and reservoirs were full. In the book of Acts, the apostles were filled over and over again with the Spirit because they were tending the lamps of their hearts.

Prayer:
Lord, fill us again and again with Your Spirit and remind us that our lamps need to be maintained in order to receive the fullness of what You have for us. Amen

Day 181

Text:
Dd Today: Pr 22 He who has a generous eye will be blessed, for he gives of his bread to the poor. He blesses us that we might be a blessing to others. ☺

Key Word:
Generous: liberal in giving or sharing; unselfish
Synonyms: generous, charitable, liberal, bountiful, munificent

Explanation:
Abraham said better than anyone else, will You bless me Lord so that I might be a blessing to others. It's only in blessing that

we will truly be blessed. When you can make someone else successful, then you are successful.

Prayer:
Will You bless us, Lord, so that we might be a blessing to others. Amen

Day 182

Text:
Dd Today: Pr 24 A wise man is strong, a man of knowledge increases strength, by wise counsel(many counselors) you will wage your own war. By yourself? NOT!! ☺

Key Word:
Many: constituting or forming a large number; numerous
Synonyms: multifarious, multitudinous, myriad

Explanation:
Once again, we are not and cannot be an island unto ourselves. A wise man once said iron sharpens iron, so one sharpens the countenance of another. We are and should be continually dependent on others to help us make our most important decisions.

Prayer:
Lord, we most certainly are dependent on You, and You also use many others around us to help us through our most desperate times. Amen

Day 183

Text:
Dd Today: Heb 9-10 Sacrifice & burnt offerings You did not desire, but through the One offering we can Boldly enter into the HoH. Faith? I think so! Yessss! ☺

Key Word:
Boldly: not hesitating or fearful in the face of actual or possible danger or rebuff; courageous and daring
Synonyms: fearless, adventurous, brave, valiant, intrepid, valorous, dauntless

Explanation:
When He (Jesus) died, the last physical sacrifice was completed and no more were required opening up the Holy of Holies for us to boldly walk into the very presence of God, unashamed. All we have to do is die to ourselves and give ourselves to Him. How, you ask? Rom 8 is very clear that we must believe in Him and confess with our mouth that He is Lord, and it will be done.

Prayer:
Lord, we believe You are who You said You are, and we confess with our mouth that Jesus is Lord. Come into our hearts today. Amen

Day 184

Text:
Dd Today: Ex 32 All the people gave Aaron their gold, he cast it in the fire & out came a calf. Be careful not to lose focus, you may end up on an idol path. ☺

Key Word:
Lose: to fail to keep, preserve, or maintain
Synonyms: expend, throw off, elude, sacrifice, dissipate, squander

Explanation:
It takes 21 days to form a habit, but it only takes a few unattended seconds to change the very course of your life.

Prayer:
Lord, keep our paths filled with variety as to keep our attention and focus on who and where it is we are going. Amen

Day 185

Text:
Dd Today: Heb 13 By Him let us continually offer the sacrifice of praise that is the fruit of our lips. By using our voice, giving thanks, God is blessed. 😊

Key Word:
Praise: the offering of grateful homage in words or song, as an act of worship
Synonyms: glorify, exalt, honor

Explanation:
I can't tell how many times I have been in a service and not felt like opening my mouth. Either my wife and I had some heated fellowship on the way to the service, or I simply didn't feel like doing it. However, all it takes is one word, and the flood gates open and the glory of the Lord pours out.
A little discipline, and you're there.

Prayer:
Pour out on us, Lord, the oil from Your throne. Honor us as lift our voice to You in a sacrifice of praise. Amen

Day 186

Text:
Dd Today: James 1 Consider it all joy, WHEN not if you encounter various trials. We will encounter trials; it is how we respond that is the key. 😊

Key Word:
When: at the time that
Synonyms: whereas, at, during

Explanation:
James knew that trials would come, thus choosing the word **when** instead of **if**. Many of us would love it if fewer trials would come, let alone the lessening of the intensity. But we all know that trials will come, and our response is what determines whether they will continue.

Prayer:
Thanks, Lord, for the trials because without them our lives would be tremendously boring. Amen

Day 187

Text:
Dd Today: James 1 Are we hearers only? Hearers are like looking in a mirror, seeing what kind of person we are, turn away & forget. Are we forgetting? ☺

Key Word:
Forgetting: to cease or fail to remember; be unable to recall
Synonyms: neglect, disregard, disremember

Explanation:
There are many times in our lives that we look into the mirror and don't like what we see, so we turn away. Instead of improving or at least taking it as a challenge to improve, we walk away discouraged and do nothing. Doing nothing only exacerbates the proble;, doing something brings His help.

Prayer:
Lord, help us to see the possibilities in the mirrors of life. Amen

Day 188

Text:
Dd Today: James 3 The tongue is an unruly member, with it we bless God & curse men. We all stumble in many things, but let it not be in word. ☺

Key Word:
Unruly: not submissive or conforming to rule; ungovernable; turbulent; intractable; refractory; lawless
Synonyms: disobedient, unmanageable, uncontrollable, stubborn, disorderly, riotous

Explanation:
God spoke, and things came into being. We are made in His image, and when we speak, we influence everything around us, both for good and bad.

Prayer:
Let the words of my mouth and the meditations of my heart be acceptable in Your sight, oh Lord. Amen

Day 189

Text:
Dd Today: Ex 39 They made the Priest's garments each piece having its own unique application. Each day we as Priests need to put on our garments for His service. ☺

Key Word:
Unique: having no like or equal; unparalleled; incomparable
Synonyms: unparalleled, extraordinary, uncommon, single

Explanation:
The priests had an outward appearance that made them look like they had everything together and functioning as it should.

Every piece of clothing had a designation and symbol. So we as priests take on the spiritual significance of each individual garment piece, but the difference being from and inward perspective instead of an outward appearance.

Prayer:
Lord, help us to be larger on the inside than the outside. Amen

Day 190

Text:
Dd Today: Ex 40 Moses built the tabernacle according to how the Lord had commanded him & the glory filled it. Let's build our lives so that we may be filled. ☺

Key Word:
Build: to establish, increase, or strengthen
Synonyms: erect, compose, originate, manufacture, heighten, fashion

Explanation:
Moses got his pattern directly from God Himself. We get our building pattern from a combination of inputs: the word, biblical teaching, and communication with the Lord. As we read, listen; as we hear, listen; as we pray, set aside time to listen.

Prayer:
Lord, You are always speaking; we ask You to interrupt our noise long enough that we may hear You. Amen

Day 191

Text:
Dd Today: Pr 4 Listen to My sayings, take care what you look upon, keep them in the midst of your heart. Guard what you hear, see, your health depends on it. ☺

Key Word:
Guard: to keep safe from harm or danger; protect; watch over
Synonyms: shield, shelter, safeguard; preserve, save

Explanation:
The Bible speaks of our eyes being a window or a gate through which we can allow good and bad to enter our soul. It is so important to guard what we see and allow into that gate. Before I was saved, I allowed lots of things to enter that should never have had that chance. The problem is after salvation we need to be especially disciplined in what we allow ourselves to look upon.

Prayer:
Be careful little eyes what you see. Help us, Lord, to keep our eye gate free from intrusion. Amen

Day 192

Text:
Dd Today: 1 Pet 2 You are a chosen generation, a royal priesthood, a holy nation, His own special people. He called us into His marvelous light. Peculiar we are! ☺

Key Word:
Peculiar: distinctive in nature or character from others, strange; queer; odd
Synonyms: individual, personal, particular, special, unique

Explanation:
When you joined this group we call Christians, you linked yourself to a very unique group indeed. The Bible calls us peculiar, and basically that means we are set apart in virtually every way: in thought, actions, words, ethics, morals, etc.

Prayer:
Lord, never let us forget who we are in You, thank You. Amen

Day 193

Text:
Dd Today: Lev 4 The people would bring their offering daily, lay their hands on it & burn it before the Lord. Let us be as faithful w/the offering of our lips. 😊

Key Word:
Offering: something offered in worship or devotion, as to a deity; an oblation or sacrifice, anything offered as a gift
Synonyms: offer, proffer, tender

Explanation:
We could learn a lot from our OT example of rituals and sacrifices. They were very disciplined and precise because the Lord gave them those procedures to follow. How much more today should we come before the Lord not with our religiosity but our willingness to give it up for Him?

Prayer:
Lord, shake us out of our religiousness leaving behind a genuine faith. Amen

Day 194

Text:
Dd Today: Pr 8 I love those who love me, & those who seek me diligently will find Me. Diligence leads to discovery, runners don't run without a purpose. 😊

Key Word:
Diligence: constant and earnest effort to accomplish what is undertaken; persistent exertion of body or mind
Synonyms: pertinacity, application, vigor, intensity

Explanation:
Those who enter a race, enter it with the sole intent of winning it or at the very least giving it all they have. All the practice and effort they have put into training for this one event is put to the test. We are in a race, but the difference is we all will be winners; however, that being said, the effort and diligence we put into that race should be the same as if there were only going to be one winner.

Prayer:
Strengthen our resolve to do the best we can possibly do while we are here in our temporary home.

Day 195

Text:
Dd Today: 1 Pet 5 Clothe yourself w/humility, God resists the proud, but gives grace to the humble. It is a voluntary action to humble oneself. Act now! ☺

Key Word:
Voluntary: done, made, brought about, undertaken, etc., of one's own accord or by free choice
Synonyms: considered, purposeful, planned, intended, designed

Explanation:
We somehow equate humility with weakness, yet in God's economy it is quite the opposite. Humility is to be honored. Chuck Swindoll mentions that it is better to serve than to be served. It seems to me someone else said the same thing.

Prayer:
Cultivate in us a servant's heart. Amen

Day 196

Text:
Dd Today: 1 Pet 5 Cast all your care-distractions, anxieties, worries & burdens of the mind, on Him, for He cares for you. Let go of stinkin thinkin! ☺

Key Word:
Cares: to have an inclination, liking, fondness, or affection
Synonyms: concern, take care, take great pains, take trouble

Explanation:
How many times have you been plagued by something and tried over and over and over to let go of it only to come to end of yourself frustrated? Then you simply lay back exhausted, relax and almost immediately an answer comes or something else happens that resolves the issue. Start with relaxing and let go.

Prayer:
Help us to realize that holding on only brings on more anxiety and that letting go brings us solutions. Amen

Day 197

Text:
Dd Today: Lev 9 Aaron & his sons presented the sacrifices as commanded by the Lord in the newly finished tabernacle. The Glory fell! Accept our sacrifice, Lord! ☺

Key Word:
Accept: to take or receive (something offered); receive with approval or favor
Synonyms: concede, acknowledge

Explanation:
In the OT if the priests didn't offer the proper sacrifices in the right way, they would be killed. Fortunately when Jesus went to the cross, He did away with the need for all the procedures and animals once for all. Now, we can come to Him openly, and He accepts us right where we are without fear of retribution.

Prayer:
Lord, help us to realize that coming to You is as easy as going to bed at night or waking up in the morning, thank You. Amen

Day 198

Text:
Dd Today: Mat 5 Let your light shine before men that they may see your good works & glorify your Father in heaven. How we walk speaks louder than how we talk. ☺

Key Word:
Shine: to be bright with reflected light; glisten; sparkle, to excel or be conspicuous
Synonyms: beam, glare, glimmer, shimmer

Explanation:
That change we all felt when we accepted Him as our Lord brought about a difference in our appearance. Our countenance was brighter, some even say it glowed. With true salvation comes a transformation is which many of the things about us change, i.e. habits, actions, reactions, speech, etc. Letting your light shine is an everyday style that allows us avenues into the lives of those around us.

Prayer:
Lord, help us to be naturally spiritual and spiritually natural. Amen

Day 199

Text:
Dd Today: Mat 6 Jesus warns us not to be 'religious'. He always responds from His heart, real and genuine. He expects nothing less of us. ☺

Key Word:
Religious: scrupulously faithful; conscientious
Synonyms: reverent, devout, pious

Explanation:
Unfortunately when Jesus mentions the religious people of the day, His context was one contrary to our above definition, indicating that they were very devout but very unscrupulous in how they approached their devotion. He would have much preferred them to be genuine and real as opposed to false and unreal.

Prayer:
Lord, create in us a clean heart, so when we approach You, we do it from a right spirit. Amen

Day 200

Text:
Dd Today: Num 22 Balaam had to be rebuked by his donkey before his eyes were opened. Paul was knocked off his. What is God saying? Open our eyes Lord. ☺

Key Word:
Open: to clear (a passage, channel, etc.) of obstructions, to give access to; make accessible or available, as for use
Synonyms: evident, plain, unimpeded, undo

Explanation:
Often times it takes some sort of catastrophic event to get our attention and move us in the direction He wants us to go. Hopefully, we will be more sensitive to His leading than a hit upside the head with a 2x4.

Prayer:
Lord, give a super sensitivity to Your HS to see with His eyes. Amen

Day 201

Text:
Dd Today: Mat 7 Let me remove the speck from your eye & look a plank is in your own. Take it from yours, then seeing clearly, help your brother. Plank eye? 😊

Key Word:
Remove: to get rid of; do away with; put an end to
Synonyms: dislodge, displace, transport

Explanation:
Before offering your own words of wisdom in any circumstance or problem, take a look at your own life and see if there is anything that might be glaring to those you're offering your words of wisdom to. We are often discredited before we can get even a word out.

Prayer:
Examine us, Lord, and see if there be any wicked in us and teach us to be blameless in all we do and say. Amen

Day 202

Text:
Dd Today: Pr 8 By me kings reign, before there ever was an earth, no depths, no fountains, before the sea was assigned its limits. Wisdom! No bounds! ☺

Key Word:
Wisdom: the quality or state of being wise; knowledge of what is true or right coupled with just judgment as to action; sagacity, discernment, or insight

Synonyms: sense, understanding, sapience, erudition, enlightenment

Explanation:
Wisdom is a quality which all of us desperately need and all of use on a daily basis whether we realize it or not.

Prayer:
If any man lacks wisdom, let him ask of God. Lord we're asking. Amen

Day 203

Text:
Dd Today: Mat 9 Jesus compares us to old & new garments, old & new wine skins. Lord, renew us w/fresh oil from your word & keep our vessels fresh & new. ☺

Key Word:
New: having but lately or but now come into knowledge
Synonyms: fresh, novel

Explanation:
There have been some interesting developments over the past 34 years that I have been serving the Lord. Terms like renewal, discipleship, slain in the spirit, restoration, seeker friendly,

etc. Some new and some old, but the one thing we need to remember is that as long as we keep our oil fresh and hold to the word of God, we will continually be alive in Him.

Prayer:
Lord, You are and that's all that matters. Amen

Day 204

Text:
Dd Today: Mat 9 She said to herself, if only I can touch His garment, I will be made well. What happens when people touch us? ☺

Key Word:
Touch: to place the hand, finger, etc., on or in contact with something
Synonyms: handle, feel

Explanation:
We have so many opportunities to touch or be touched by Him. I can remember services in which His presence was so thick all you had to do was reach out and touch Him. Other occasions, we would pray for individuals or be in counseling sessions, and He would use us to touch them and heal them. We serve such an incredibly awesome God.

Prayer:
Lord, make us a vessel from which Your touch can be easily accessed. Amen

Day 205

Text:
Dd Today: Mat 11 Jesus said, come to Me, all who labor & are heavy laden & I will give you rest. Jesus, not a body builder, but definitely a weight lifter. ☺

Key Word:
Rest: relief or freedom, esp. from anything that wearies, troubles, or disturbs
Synonyms: stop, halt, standstill

Explanation:
I think that in most instances we need to do as the synonyms here indicate. We need to stop, halt or standstill for a moment in order to get some real life perspective on our situation. We live in such a fast-paced world today, often the simple act of stopping what we're doing and taking a deep breath gives us a chance to reflect.

Prayer:
As we run, run, run through life, help us to stop and take time to be with You. Amen

Day 206

Text:
Dd Today: Pr 12 Anxiety in the heart of a man causes depression, but a good word makes it glad. Not only what we say, but how we say it can bring deliverance. ☺

Key Word:
Glad: feeling joy or pleasure; delighted; pleased
Synonyms: merry, joyous, joyful, cheerful, happy, cheery

Explanation:
I know, and my wife will verify, that there have been so many times when I have said something to her in a matter of fact way and she would get hurt. I really didn't understand why until I began to read about communicating. It wasn't what I said at all, it was the <u>way</u> I said it. Words are very powerful, and the way we use them is critical as to their ultimate impact.

Prayer:
Thank You, Lord, for making our words such a dynamic force and help us to be sensitive as to their use in impacting others lives. Amen

Day 207

Text:
Dd Today: Mat 12 Jesus speaks of good trees bearing good fruit. Sometimes we need to check the state of our tree so that the fruit thereof is worth eating. ☺

Key Word:
State: the condition of a person or thing, as with respect to circumstances or attributes
Synonyms: condition, situation, status

Explanation:
I have visited many churches over the years and spoken with a lot of different kinds of people. In virtually every case you can determine or see the place they are in by observing the resultant fruit and/or lack thereof.

Prayer:
Lord, examine our lives and help us to be fruit bearers as well as fruit pickers. Amen

Day 208

Text:
Dd Today: Mat 13 The Bible speaks of our heart being like soil, Jesus taught about 3 kinds of soil. How we prepare the soil determines our crop. ☺

Key Word:
Prepare: to put in proper condition or readiness
Synonyms: provide, arrange, order

Explanation:
Growing up on a small farm, tending gardens and planting seeds, I understood the importance of preparing the soil in order to get the best possible harvest. So it is with our hearts; if not prepared and cultivated properly, we will reap a harvest of whatever is sown.

Prayer:
Dig us deep, Lord, and prepare our soil so that our harvest will be plentiful. Amen

Day 209

Text:
Dd Today: Pr 15 A soft answer turns away wrath, but harsh words stirs up anger. Our response will be received much better than our reaction. 😊

Key Word:
Soft: smooth, soothing, or ingratiating
Synonyms: mellifluous, dulcet, sweet, tender, sympathetic

Explanation:
My wife is excellent at this; she has had some very serious confrontations over the years, which if she had not responded with a soft answer could have escalated into something quite different than the result she got.

Prayer:
In the times we want to react, help us to respond in such a way as to diffuse what otherwise might be a sticky situation. Amen

Day 210

Text:
Dd Today: Pr 16 Commit your works to the Lord & your thoughts will be established. Let's purposefully take steps toward right thinking. 😊

Key Word:
Established: to show to be valid or true; prove
Synonyms: verify, substantiate

Explanation:
Think of a time when you disagreed with someone or something and instead of giving an explanation, you just went off in your thinking down some rabbit trail that left you angry and mad about the whole situation. Taking it to the Lord will always bring a settling instead of an uprising.

Prayer:
Lord, we commit our thoughts to You; help us to discipline our minds to think Phil 4 thoughts. Amen

Day 211

Text:
Dd Today: Num 9 The people followed the Lord, a cloud by day & a pillar of fire by night. Let's open our eyes wide enough to see where He is leading. 😊

Key Word:
See: to be cognizant of; recognize
Synonyms: observe, notice, distinguish, discern, behold, regard

Explanation:
Even the Israelites, who had manna, clothes that never wore out, the Red Sea parting, cloud by day, pillar of fire by night,

still lost their focus when their leader was out of view. These were physically visible things. It is so obvious to us reading the story and looking back, but what about the rest of today, tomorrow, next week, next year?

Prayer:
With all the distractions we have in our world today, help us to stop, take time to gain and keep Your perspective. Amen

Day 212

Text:
Dd Today: Num 10 As Israel set out the Lord gave them a promise. I will give it to you...for the Lord has promised good things for you. Stand on your promise. 😊

Key Word:
Promise: something that has the effect of an express assurance; indication of what may be expected
Synonyms: pledge, covenant, agree

Explanation:
When Linda and I got married, we gave each other a promise that we would love, honor and cherish each other so long as we both should live. I know she has lived up to her side of the bargain, but I certainly haven't always lived up to mine. The one thing we can count on is that the Lord will always live up to His.

Prayer:
Thank You for the many promises we have from You and that You always live up to them. Amen

Day 213

Text:
Dd Today: Num 11 The people complained about their situation, longing for the fineries of Egypt. Looking back is never an option, ask Lot's wife. On we go! ☺

Key Word:
Longing: strong, persistent desire or craving, esp. for something unattainable or distant
Synonyms: aspiration, desirous, yearning

Explanation:
Everyone says the hindsight is always 20/20; however, in this circumstance, the Israelites were only falling back on what they knew and were not trusting in the promises the Lord had given them. It is that false sense of security that tends to draw us back to something familiar rather than pressing on into the promise land.

Prayer:
Lord, help us to see beyond our nose and to follow Your banner no matter what the circumstances look like or how familiar the past is. Amen

Day 214

Text:
Dd Today: Pr 21 There is no wisdom or understanding or counsel against the Lord. Our first line of defense is always Him, never our last resort. ☺

Key Word:
Against: in opposition to; contrary to; adverse or hostile to
Synonyms: opposing, contrary, versus

Explanation:
David said to run into the Lord for He is a shield and buckler, a very present help in a time of trouble. We, unfortunately, will never be totally free of trouble, but if we can learn to exhaust His resources first and not ours, we will be a great deal more successful in dealing with them.

Prayer:
I put my trust in You, Lord, first and foremost. Amen

Day 215

Text:
Dd Today: Rev 21 It is done. I am the alpha & the omega, the beginning & the end. I will give the fountain, the water of life freely to him who thirsts. Thirsty? 😊

Key Word:
Thirsts: strong or eager desire; craving
Synonyms: craving, passion, drought, wish, hunger

Explanation:
When I think of the idea of thirsting after God, I compare it to coming out of the desert after days and days of no water, so dry that the smallest drop is absolutely and incomprehensibly wonderful.

Prayer:
Ignite our passion and thirst for You, Lord, as if we were just emerging from the desert. Amen

Day 216

Text:
Dd Today: Num 14 Of those who complained against the Lord re: the spies report of the land, they could not enter, but those of faith went in. Hear w/faith! 😊

Key Word:
Complained: to express dissatisfaction, pain, uneasiness, censure, resentment, or grief; find fault

Synonyms: complain, grumble, growl, whine are terms for expressing dissatisfaction or discomfort

Explanation:
Most of the people at that juncture in their wonderings could not see beyond what was in front of them in spite of the Lord's provision. Faith requires us to look past our circumstances and current situations, letting Him be our eyes and ears looking to the promises He gave us.

Prayer:
Lord, allow us to see and hear through Your eyes and ears. Amen

Day 217

Text:
Dd Today: Num 15 Thank God we no longer have to go to the priest w/the proper offering to be forgiven. We now have direct access to His throne. Call today! 😊

Key Word:
Direct: without intervening persons, influences, factors, etc.; immediate; personal

Synonyms: beeline, linear, straight, unswerving

Explanation:
Once Jesus died and the veil was rent in the Temple, we have direct access to the very presence that only a few could experience in the days of the Tabernacle. We can walk into the most holy place and speak with Him as our Father, our friend.

Prayer:
Thank You, Lord, for opening up the veil for us to experience a close and personal relationship with You and the Father. Amen

Day 218

Text:
Dd Today: Pr 25 Take away the dross from the silver it will go to the silversmith for jewelry. Let Him turn up the heat, we all need to be in the master's hand. ☺

Key Word:
Dross: The scum that forms on the surface of molten metal as a result of oxidation
Synonyms: scum, impurities, dregs, refuse, sediment

Explanation:
The only way we can be purified is for Him to turn up the heat in our lives through various relationships, circumstances, etc., which will bring to the surface the impurities in our character, and once there, He can skim them off.

Prayer:
Turn up the heat, Lord, and begin to skim off those traits we need to leave behind. Amen

Day 219

Text:
Dd Today: Num 17 Moses gathered 12 rods from all the tribes. Aaron's put forth blossoms & almonds. Let's not test the Lord & obey Him the first time. ☺

Key Word:
Test: the means by which the presence, quality, or genuineness of anything is determined; a means of trial

Synonyms: assay, prove, examine

Explanation:
The only thing we are to test God in is our tithes and offerings. Other than that, He tests us.

Prayer:
With You, Lord, there is no final exam, You are way more interested in our character than our comfort. Continue to test us so that the process moves on. Amen

Day 220

Text:
Dd Today: Pr 26 Like the legs of the lame that hang limp, is a proverb in the mouth of fools. Let's always be ready w/a right word, guarding our mouth. 😊

Key Word:
Right: in accordance with what is good, proper, or just
Synonyms: accurate, true, fit, seemly, proper

Explanation:
I think the key here is to make sure we think before we speak with the realization that our words can be truly life or death in any given situation.

Prayer:
Teach us to use and choose our words wisely. Amen

Day 221

Text:
Dd Today: Mat 3 John came preaching repentance w/ authority, yet he stood down when Jesus came to him. We have authority, but humility gives us credibility. 😊

Key Word:
Credibility: worthy of belief or confidence; trustworthy
Synonyms: plausible, likely, reasonable, tenable

Explanation:
We must remember that the authority we have is only as good as the character behind it. We all know what a man without character looks and feels like. Let's not be found in the same breath.

Prayer:
Lord, thank You for the authority You have given us. Help us to be good stewards and not abuse it. Amen

Day 222

Text:
Dd Today: Mat 4 Satan proved he knows the word in his tempting Jesus who used it skillfully against him. When it comes to the word, are we inept or adept? 😊

Key Word:
Adept: very skilled; proficient; expert
Synonyms: savvy, accomplished, skillful, master, proficient

Explanation:
We must remember that Satan is very competent when it comes to the Word and will twist it to his advantage whenever possible, thus the need for us to be adept and learned in the Word so as not to fall for his traps.

Prayer:
As we are faithful in Your word, quicken it to us in a very practical and applicable way. Amen

Day 223

Text:
Dd Today: Pr 16 He who is slow to anger is better than the mighty & he who rules his spirit than he who takes a city. Strength is not in might, but in decision. ☺

Key Word:
Decision: the quality of being decided; firmness
Synonyms: volition, conclusion, firmness, fortitude

Explanation:
There is something about a man who is decisive and disciplined. We have had many people speak into our lives over the years, and it is always the character behind the words that many times is more impactful than the words themselves.

Prayer:
Lord, help us to live what we believe every day in order to lend credibility to our words. Amen

Day 224

Text:
Dd Today: Mat 15 We are told that out of the heart the mouth speaks. What we allow ourselves to see, hear & think can & will...you finish it!! ☺

Key Word:
Allow: to permit by neglect, oversight, or the like
Synonyms: allow, let, permit

Explanation:
Regardless of how much we think we can allow such things as movies, TV, lyrics, internet, etc. into our lives, we very much have to govern the thinking and speech patterns that are generated from there.

Prayer:
Help us put a filter on our eyes, ears and mouth when we come into contact with most of the world. Amen

Day 225

Text:
Dd Today: Num 33 Moses told the people that when they entered the land, they were to drive out all the inhabitants of the land. Who occupies your land? Huh? 😊

Key Word:
Drive out: force to go away
Synonyms: chase away, dispel, run off

Explanation:
We are to drive out all the inhabitants of the land because if we fail to, they will come back to haunt us later on as they did the Israelites.

Prayer:
Show us the inhabitants of our land just as You did the Israelites and then go before us as we go in to possess it. Amen

Day 226

Text:
Dd Today: Mat 18 Assuredly, I say to you, unless you are converted & become as little children... Remember, we are to become childlike not childish. 😊

Key Word:
Converted: to change in character; cause to turn from an evil life to a righteous one
Synonyms: reformed, changed, indoctrinated, transformed

Explanation:
Jesus loved little children because they had an innocence about them that didn't involve facades or anything pretentious. They would accept knowing with confidence that it would be ok.

Prayer:
Lord, in faith, I come to You as a little child with no assumptions, trusting You will be and do exactly what You said you would. Amen

Day 227

Text:
Dd Today: Pr 20 The spirit of a man is the lamp of the Lord, searching all the inner depths of his heart. Remember He IS the ultimate PI. Unlock your doors. ☺

Key Word:
Unlock: to open or release by or as if by undoing a lock
Synonyms: unbutton, unravel, undo, liberate, unfasten, free

Explanation:
As we begin to open up to the Lord, He will be faithful to reveal to us the areas which need tweaking. Fortunately for us, in His revelation, He gently prompts us to let go of whatever it is we need to let go of.

Prayer:
Lord, we give You the key to the inner recesses of our heart, those closets that have been shut for possibly long periods of time. Open the door and bring healing as well as surgically remove those areas that need it. Amen

Day 228

Text:
Dd Today: Mat 18 Peter asked how many times he should forgive, Jesus told him as many times as it takes. Forgiveness is as much for the forgiver as the forgivee. ☺

Key Word:
Forgive: to cease to feel resentment against
Synonyms: excuse, absolve, acquit

Explanation:
In Peter's case, he was thinking (in his humanness) a finite number of times in which he should forgive; however, the Lord quickly corrected him and adjusted his thinking to a number which would shatter the box of his thinking. Unforgiveness ties us to the person it is directed towards while forgiveness cuts those ties and therefore releases both parties.

Prayer:
Lord, bring to our mind those whom we need to forgive and cut those ties that have both of us bound. Amen

Day 229

Text:
Dd Today: Num 35 Just like a city of refuge, we can run to the Lord and be safe, under the shadow of His wings. Outside of Him we are open to attack. ☺

Key Word:
Refuge: a place of shelter, protection, or safety
Synonyms: security, safety, asylum, retreat, sanctuary, haven, stronghold

Explanation:
In the OT they had six cities they could run to in case of some unforeseen event or occurrence. They would receive protection and sanctuary there as long as they remained in one of the cities. In our case we can run to the Lord, and He provides us an umbrella of protection, i.e. fathers over families, the church, parents over children, etc. The same applies if we leave His protection. We are vulnerable to attack without Him.

Prayer:
Thank You for Your protection and never let us take it for granted. Amen

Day 230

Text:
Dd Today: Pr 23 Do not remove the ancient landmarks, those things which point you toward the living God. They will keep you on the right path. 😊

Key Word:
Landmark: a boundary line indicated by a stone, stake, etc. Landmarks could not be removed without incurring the severe displeasure of God.
Synonyms: milestone, watershed, benchmark

Explanation:
When the ancients had a breakthrough or some sort of life changing event, i.e. conquering land, God speaking, anything that would change the course of their fortunes, they would set up an altar or erect some sort of monument to the event so that every time they saw it, they would remember God's faithfulness. We are no different today in that we need to remember those life-changing events that lead us to where we are in Christ.

Prayer:
Thank You, Lord, for Your faithfulness, You did not bring us out this far for us to simply turn back. Amen

Day 231

Text:
Dd Today: Mat 19 Trusting in man will always disappoint, but Jesus said all things are possible with God. ☺

Key Word:
Possible: capable of happening, existing, or being true
Synonyms: obtainable, practicable, probable, promising

Explanation:
Many years ago, we put our trust more in the church and a leader than in God. Needless to say, we ended up completely devastated, but God was not a God of devastation, but a God of restoration. We learned firsthand how much our God really loved us and that we should put our trust in Him not in him.

Prayer:
We trust You, Lord, no matter what happens, we will always put our trust in You. Amen

Day 232

Text:
Dd Today: Deut 6 The greatest commandment, you shall love the Lord your God w/all your heart, w/all your soul, & w/all you strength. It's all Yours, SSB! ☺

Key Word:
Greatest: remarkable or outstanding in magnitude, degree, or extent
Synonyms: immense, enormous, gigantic, huge, vast, grand

Explanation:
Jesus said the greatest commandment was this one. What more do we need to know? Put your spirit, soul, and body into it and see what the result will be.

Prayer:
You are always worthy of all our love. Amen

Day 233

Text:
Dd Today: Pr 30 Every word of God is pure; He is a shield to those who put their trust in Him. Do not add to His words. Don't put words in His mouth!! ☺

Key Word:
Pure: free from anything of a different, inferior, or contaminating kind; free from extraneous matter

Synonyms: unmixed, unadulterated, unalloyed, uncontaminated, immaculate

Explanation:
Sometimes we like to embellish on stories or events or circumstances, but God is quite different in that regard. He has written it out and even warns us not to do any of those things.

Prayer:
We take You at Your word, Lord, and commit to never exaggerate or say anything that might add to or take away from what You said. Amen

Day 234

Text:
Dd Today: Deut 7 For you are a holy people...a special treasure above all the peoples on the face of the earth. Keep us mindful of how You see us. ☺

Key Word:
Special: of a distinct or particular kind or character
Synonyms: uncommon, unique

Explanation:
I think we would all do ourselves a favor by stepping back and letting the Lord give us His particular rendition of us.

Prayer:
I am so grateful for Your perspective of me, Lord. Amen

Day 235

Text:
Dd Today: Mk 1 The disciples were both casting their nets to catch & mending their nets to keep. The kingdom is not into catch & release, but catch & keep. ☺

Key Word:
Catch: to intercept and seize; take and hold
Synonyms: apprehend, arrest

Explanation:
Jesus knew what He was doing when He chose fisherman as His disciples. These were folks who not only knew how to cast and catch, but also were very good at and understood the necessity of mending their nets in order to keep what they caught. Not all were good at catching and not all were good at mending, but both very necessary when it comes to building the church.

Prayer:
Lord, help us to see how we can best serve the body in both catching and keeping what is caught. Amen

Day 236

Text:
Dd Today: Mk 2 And He said to Levi, 'follow Me'. So he arose & followed Him. Would those 2 words be enough for us walk away from all we are doing? ☺

Key Word:
Follow: to accept as a guide or leader; accept the authority of or give allegiance to
Synonyms: obey, heed, observe, accompany, attend

Explanation:
We all have received this call from Him. To what degree are we heeding the call we were given? The call is purely individual and specific to each of us. We must determine what it is we are called to and function accordingly.

Prayer:
Lord, thank You for calling us out of our former lives and putting our feet upon the Rock. Strengthen us in Your calling for our lives so that we may fulfill our purpose in You. Amen

Day 237

Text:
Dd Today: Pr 3 In all your ways have direct, intimate contact w/Him & He shall make straight & right your paths. Nuff said!!! ☺

Key Word:
Straight: without a bend, angle, or curve; not curved; direct
Synonyms: plumb, honorable, lineal

Explanation:
If we will take daily time with Him, quality time, we will have no choice but to walk according to the path shown to us. We will know Him, and He will be able to communicate with us.

Prayer:
Create is us a desire to get closer to You so that we will be better able to discern Your path. Amen

Day 238

Text:
Dd Today: Mk 3 No one can enter a strong man's house & plunder his goods, unless he 1st binds the strong man. Jesus gives us power to bind & loose. Go for it! ☺

Key Word:
Bind: to tie up
Synonyms: confine, restrain

Explanation:
Almost all of us have strongholds that we need to bind and loose in our lives. I know I had a very real fear of man that was and still does from time to time keeping me from being confident and bold. Once I bound it up and cast it aside, basically faced it head on, a weight was lifted off my shoulders.

Prayer:
Lord, show us those areas in our lives we need to bind and loose so we can be free in You. Amen

Day 239

Text:
Dd Today: Pr 4:23-27 Consider your heart, eyes, mouth & feet; monitor your behavior, using self control & discipline. For it will only do you good, always. ☺

Key Word:
Consider: to think carefully about, esp. in order to make a decision; contemplate; reflect on
Synonyms: ponder, deliberate, weigh, study

Explanation:
I had a very wise boss one time who always said, "it can look right and be wrong, but very seldom can it look wrong and be right." We should always stay as far away from those things that look wrong as possible and never say ok just to go along.

Prayer:
Lord, pierce our conscience so we always make our yes, yes and our no, no. Amen

Day 240

Text:
Dd Today: Mk 5 Before Jesus healed the ruler of the synagogue's daughter he said, "do not be afraid; only believe". Belief - fear = results!!! ☺

Key Word:
Afraid: feeling fear; filled with apprehension
Synonyms: scared, fearful, disquieted, apprehensive, timid

Explanation:
James said it very plainly, without fear and doubting. If we can leave those two out of the equation, then results will shortly follow.

Prayer:
Lord, as Your disciples once asked You, help our unbelief? Thank You, Amen

Day 241

Text:
Dd Today: Apr 6 The Lord chose, in His infinite wisdom, to have my beautiful, awesome, talented, gorgeous bride born on this day. HAPPY BIRTHDAY SWEETIE!!! ☺

Key Word:
Gorgeous: splendid or sumptuous in appearance, coloring, etc.; magnificent
Synonyms: rich, superb, grand; brilliant, resplendent, glittering, dazzling

Explanation:
She is all of the above.

Prayer:
Lord, please bless my wife on her day to come into this world. Amen

Day 242

Text:
Dd Today: Mk 7 Jesus said many things including, "if anyone has an ear to hear, let him hear!" Lord, dig our ears deep that we never fail to hear. ☺

Key Word:
Hear: to listen to; give or pay attention to
Synonyms: attend, regard, heed, listen

Explanation:
So many times we are distracted with our own thoughts that we think we are listening, but it's in one ear and out the other. Let's do our best to quiet ourselves so we can really attend to, heed, or regard what He is saying.

Prayer:
Thanks, Lord, for speaking, we will do our best to listen. Amen

Day 243

Text:
Dd Today: Pr 8 I was there before there was ever an earth, before depths, before fountains, before the primal dust. Who am I? Wisdom, find Me, find life! ☺

Key Word:
Before: in front of; ahead of; in advance of
Synonyms: fore, forehand, formerly

Explanation:
Wisdom in not something you get in an instant. It is an acquired taste, and like wine, gets better and better over time.

Prayer:
Like James, we want the wisdom from above. Please give us wisdom beyond our years. Amen

Day 244

Text:
Dd Today: Pr 9 Do not correct a scoffer, lest he hate you, rebuke a wise man and he will love you. What do we do when correction comes? Respond or react! ☺

Key Word:
Rebuke: sharp, stern disapproval; reproof; reprimand
Synonyms: censure, upbraid, chide, admonish

Explanation:
I know there have been times when I have received correction that I knew it wasn't the right thing to do at the time, but with

my blood pressure rising, I bit my lip and thanked the person delivering it. Thinking all the while, Lord, what would You have me learn from this? Other times I wasn't quite so gracious.

Prayer:
Help us, Lord, to always recognize a rebuke or correction as an opportunity to learn or grow. Amen

Day 245

Text:
Dd Today: Mk 9 If you can believe, all things are possible. Lord, we believe, help our unbelief. In the shy side of our faith we say help our unbelief. ☺

Key Word:
Unbelief: the state or quality of not believing; incredulity or skepticism, esp. in matters of doctrine or religious faith
Synonyms: incredulity, discredit, incredulousness

Explanation:
When I look at many of the happenings, i.e. blind eyes opened, the dead raised up, bones healed, hearing restored in third world countries, I know it is due to their childlike acceptance of what the Lord can do that enables such things to take place.

Prayer:
Lord, break down our barriers and breakthrough our walls into the miraculous. Amen

Day 246

Text:
Dd Today: Mk 9 Everyone will be proven w/fire & every sacrifice seasoned w/salt. Fire purifies, salt preserves from corruption. Let the flame keep us salty. ☺

Key Word:
Proven: having been demonstrated or verified without doubt
Synonyms: demonstrate, confirm, substantiate, verify

Explanation:
Have you ever noticed that after you have taught, given advice, or exhorted someone that the Lord tends to challenge that area of your life? No coincidence here!

Prayer:
Go ahead and prove us, Lord. It will only make us better. Amen

Day 247

Text:
Dd Today: 2 Ch 7 Solomon prayed, fire came, consumed the sacrifice, His glory filled the temple. As we pray, His desire is to fill this temple over & over. ☺

Key Word:
Filled: to supply or provide to the fullest extent
Synonyms: crowd, pack, jam, cram

Explanation:
In the book of Acts, the disciples were filled over and over again with the HS, who gave them the words they were to use, the anointing to heal, earthquakes to release and so on.

Prayer:
Consume our sacrifice, Lord, and fill us again and again. Amen

Day 248

Text:
Dd Today: Mk 10 With men it is impossible, but w/God all things are possible. Dreams are from the heart of God. Let your faith fuel your dreams. ☺

Key Word:
Dreams: an aspiration; goal; aim
Synonyms: vision, creativity, design

Explanation:
The Psalmist said it correctly. He gives us the desires of our heart, or maybe better said, He puts His desires or dreams for us into our heart.

Prayer:
Lord, put Your desires in our heart and our visions will line up. Amen

Day 249

Text:
Dd Today: Pr 17 The beginning of strife is like releasing water, therefore stop contention before a quarrel starts. Close the spillway before the dam breaks. 😊

Key Word:
Stop: to cause to cease; put an end to
Synonyms: arrest, check, halt

Explanation:
Before we speak, if we consider whether we are part of the problem or part of the solution, it will be harder for us to continue and possibly exacerbate an already escalated situation.

Prayer:
Lord, help us to be slow to speak and even slower to listen to anything that even resembles gossip. Amen

Day 250

Text:
Dd Today: Pr 18 Death & life are in the power of the tongue & those who love it will eat its fruit. Love it and eat it!!! ☺

Key Word:
Eat: to consume by or as if by devouring gradually; wear away; corrode
Synonyms: devour, gorge, squander

Explanation:
I once spent about a month in Mexico, and not knowing the language very well, I could speak well enough to get myself into a whole lot of trouble but not get out of it. We must use our brain and our heart before we speak so that our words are a gift to the hearer.

Prayer:
Lord, let our words be a gift to all those who are within earshot. Amen

Day 251

Text:
Dd Today: Lk 1 As John was a voice preparing the way of the Lord. So when we speak, is it in such a way as to prepare the heart of the hearer? ☺

Key Word:
Prepare: to put things or oneself in readiness; get ready
Synonyms: provide, arrange, order

Explanation:
The way we speak and conduct ourselves has a great deal to do with the receptiveness of those around us. My sister once told

me that the whole family has been watching my life since I got saved and has been very impressed with the fruit of it.

Prayer:
Lord, let our lives be a living testimony to the wonderful things you have done in and through us. Amen

Day 252

Text:
Dd Today: Pr 22 Do not remove the ancient landmark which your fathers have set. Never take for granted the events which moved you forward in God. Remember? ☺

Key Word:
Remember: to retain in the memory; keep in mind; remain aware of
Synonyms: recall, recollect

Explanation:
Jesus said do this in remembrance of Me, undisputedly the most recognized act in the history of mankind. Each one of us have events that have occurred throughout our lives that have shaped us. All we have to do is remember.

Prayer:
As we reflect on those events that molded our lives, help us to see them in Your light. Amen

Day 253

Text:
Dd Today: Lk 4 They were astonished at His teaching, for His word was with authority. He also gave us that same authority. If only we believe! So simple. ☺

Key Word:
Authority: the power to determine, adjudicate, or otherwise settle issues or disputes; jurisdiction; the right to control, command, or determine
Synonyms: rule, power, sway, control, influence

Explanation:
I don't think that most of us realize the authority we have in Christ. When He sent out the disciples and gave them authority, they came back to Him with reports of all kinds of healings, deliverance, spirits obeying them, etc. He has released that same authority to us, believe it.

Prayer:
Show us Your power. Lord, use us. Amen

Day 254

Text:
Dd Today: Deut 28 IF you will obey the Lord & observe all His statutes, then all these blessings will overtake you. IF becomes a VERY big word. 😊

Key Word:
Overtake: to catch up with and pass, as in a race; move by
Synonyms: outdistance, overwhelm, catch up

Explanation:
If is a conditional term, and we have to meet certain criteria in order for the Lord to honor the then portion of the commitment. We hold up our end, and He will hold up His.

Prayer:
Lord, help us to realize the gravity of If. Amen

Day 255

Text:
Dd Today: Deut 29 He led them 40 yrs in the wilderness, their clothes & sandals never wore out, He provided their every need. Do you think He...nah, not us? ☺

Key Word:
Provided: to furnish; supply
Synonyms: give, render, produce

Explanation:
If we would look around us long enough to appreciate all that He has provided for us, we would begin to have a better appreciation of exactly how involved He is in our daily lives.

Prayer:
Lord, help be aware of the little things that make our lives what they are. Amen

Day 256

Text:
Dd Today: Lk 6 Love your enemies, do good, for He is kind to the unthankful & evil. Amazing, we are to treat the ungrateful with kindness. Imagine that! ☺

Key Word:
Kind: having, showing, or proceeding from benevolence
Synonyms: mild, benign, benignant, gentle, tender, compassionate

Explanation:
Most of the time we feel like tearing into those who do evil. I'm talking about rape, molestation, mutilation, and those who are simply ungrateful for things that are done for them. Well, Jesus puts it this way, we should be nice to them, bless them,

and even forgive them. That doesn't mean there aren't any consequences for their actions, but how else are they going to tangibly see the love of God?

Prayer:
Let Your blessings rain down on the just and the unjust. Amen

Day 257

Text:
Dd Today: Deut 30 But the word is very near you, in your mouth & in your heart. He put it there so we would Love Him with All our heart. Let someone know! ☺

Key Word:
Near: close; to a point or place not far away
Synonyms: imminent, impending, approaching

Explanation:
The Lord said He wrote the wWord on the tablets of our hearts, so really all we have to do is let the Holy Spirit bring it to us in our everyday conversations. We read it every day to remind us it is there.

Prayer:
Thanks, Lord, for be so generous in giving us Your word both in written and indelibly imprinted on our hearts. Amen

Day 258

Text:
Dd Today: Pr 27 As in water face reflects face, so a man's heart reveals the man. Invite the HS to take a look, He'll improve your face value. ☺

Key Word:
Reflect: to think, ponder, or meditate
Synonyms: ruminate, deliberate, muse, consider, cogitate, contemplate

Explanation:
When I read the Word, many times I see it jump off the page, and there's a connection and reflection of myself and just how I have been lately. I am forced at that point to consider myself as if I was looking into a mirror. It is at that moment that I know if I will invite Him to take a look, He will be faithful to help me with whatever it is His light is focused on.

Prayer:
Lord, help us to go be open to Your examination of any area in our lives. Amen

Day 259

Text:
Dd Today: Lk 8 The woman came with only a hope of touching His garment & went away healed. Often out of desperation & expectation the realization comes. ☺

Key Word:
Realization: the making or being made real of something imagined, planned, etc
Synonyms: fulfillment, materialization, actualization

Explanation:
When we come to end of our rope, He is always there with an extension.

Prayer:
Thank You, Lord, for always coming through. Amen

Day 260

Text:
Dd Today: Pr 29 A man's pride will bring him low, but the humble in spirit will retain honor. Humility = you - pride! The lower you is better!! ☺

Key Word:
Retain: to continue to hold or have
Synonyms: hold, preserve

Explanation:
Pride is always associated with destruction in the Word. The further you can keep from it, the better.

Prayer:
Make us as David was a man after God's own heart, keeping his own heart contrite. Amen

Day 261

Text:
Dd Today: Pr 30 Every word of God is pure; He is a shield to those who put their trust in Him. We must PUT(action word) our trust in Him. Protection follows. ☺

Key Word:
Put: to assign or attribute
Synonyms: place, lay, set

Explanation:
I think the emphasis here is on the action of doing something, putting effort into it and seeing the result confirmed.

Prayer:
Once again as David said, "I put my trust in You, oh Lord." Amen

Day 262

Text:
Dd Today: Deut 34 Moses, whom the Lord knew face to face. Jesus opened the way for us to have that kind of intimacy with the Lord. Is that our desire? ☺

Key Word:
Intimacy: a close, familiar, and usually affectionate or loving personal relationship with another person or group
Synonyms: closeness, familiarity, warmth, affection

Explanation:
I set aside time every day to be with Him, no matter how long it is. He truly is my friend, and I can tell Him anything or nothing- just being there with Him is enough.

Prayer:
Truly one day in Your courts is better than 1,000 elsewhere. Amen

Day 263

Text:
Dd Today: Josh 1 The Lord spoke to Joshua, Moses my servant is dead. I say to you the old life is gone, go & possess your land. Go & Possess Your land. ☺

Key Word:
Go: to move or proceed, esp. to or from something
Synonyms: walk, run, travel, advance

Explanation:
Joshua was told to 'go', the disciples were told to 'go', we are told to 'go'. Maybe we should 'go'.

Prayer:
Lord, in confidence and faith we 'go'. Amen

Day 264

Text:
Dd Today: Pr 4 Get wisdom & understanding, when you walk your steps won't be hindered, when you run you will not stumble. Let us keep our eyes on the prize. ☺

Key Word:
Hindered: to obstruct or delay the progress of
Synonyms: encumber, obstruct, trammel, block, thwart

Explanation:
When we walk in wisdom and with understanding, our eyes open up to see the pitfalls of our path so that we can very easily avoid falling into them.

Prayer:
Thank You, Lord, for the wisdom You give us every day to make those key decision we encounter. Amen

Day 265

Text:
Dd Today: Josh 6 Even though the Lord may ask us to do something a bit different, walk around the city 7 times & shout, if we are faithful He will be also. ☺

Key Word:
Different: not ordinary; unusual
Synonyms: unlike, diverse, divergent, contrary

Explanation:
There have been times when the Lord asked me to do something that was quite different than I would have done like start a church in a small town in eastern Oregon, but I did it out of obedience, and the blessing was definitely there.

Prayer:
Even though it may sound weird, we'll do it anyway. Amen

Day 266

Text:
Dd Today: Josh 7 Josh threw himself before the Lord & He put His finger on the sin in the camp. When He puts His finger on our life, do we do as Josh did? ☺

Key Word:
Threw: to cause to fall to the ground, esp. to hurl to the ground
Synonyms: launch, send

Explanation:
Will we allow Him to put His finger on any area of our lives? I know I have sometimes resisted opening certain areas to His leading, and my resistance is always met with the consequences of my resistance.

Prayer:
Lord, see if there be any wicked in me and lead me into thy everlasting life. Amen

Day 267

Text:
Dd Today: Josh 7 Achan fell to temptation & took things under the ban causing his whole family to perish. All of us are tempted; it's how we handle it. ☺

Key Word:
Tempt: to entice or allure to do something often regarded as unwise, wrong, or immoral
Synonyms: tantalize, instigate, risk, dare

Explanation:
When we don't take care of hidden sin or even habits that can lead us in wrong direction, it not only affects us, but will also eventually come back on the family.

Prayer:
Opening up to You our weaknesses and strengths can be the best thing that ever happen to us and our families. Help us to be open, Lord. Amen

Day 268

Text:
Dd Today: Lk 19 Jesus' story of the ten minas is related to our talents. We are all given various talents, what are you doing with yours? ☺

Key Word:
Talent: a special natural ability or aptitude
Synonyms: capability, gift, genius

Explanation:
Unlike many others in my younger days, I tried to maximize my athletic abilities to be the best that I could be. Many of us are dripping with talent of one form or another; the key is to find out what they are and to use them to their fullest.

Prayer:
Lord, make us an instrument in Your hand playing us to our fullest. Amen

Day 269

Text:
Dd Today: Josh 10 Joshua had barely conquered Jericho & Ai when 5 Amorite kings came up against him. Satan will always come, but it is the Lord Who delivers. ☺

Key Word:
Deliver: to set free or liberate
Synonyms: redeem, rescue

Explanation:
After a victory, our accuser doesn't take a vacation; in fact he doesn't rest. The great thing is with the Lord, we never have to question our deliverance.

Prayer:
Help us to be sensitive to Your working in our everyday lives, so we can tangibly see Your deliverance. Amen

Day 270

Text:
Dd Today: Pr 13 He who guards his mouth preserves his life, but he who opens his lips shall have destruction. Are your words, a messenger of life or death? ☺

Key Word:
Preserves: to keep safe from harm or injury; protect or spare
Synonyms: safeguard, shelter, shield

Explanation:
Our words are very powerful things, and most of us don't realize just how influential they can be. God knows that He has to watch everything He says because literally everything He says comes to be. Why should we be any less careful?

Prayer:
Lord, help us to realize the gravity of our words every day. Amen

Day 271

Text:
Dd Today: Josh 11 Joshua utterly destroyed his enemies as the Lord had commanded. The Lord wants us to utterly destroy our enemies. Take no captives! ☺

Key Word:
Utterly: in an utter manner; completely; absolutely
Synonyms: entirely, fully, wholly, totally

Explanation:
Compromise wasn't an option for the Israelites. Why should it be for us? Take a look at what it did for them, and you will understand just why He told them not to.

Prayer:
Lord, never let us settle for second best. Amen

Day 272

Text:
Dd Today: Pr 17 Wisdom is in the presence of one who has understanding, but the eyes of a fool are on the ends of the earth. Stay focused on what is at hand. ☺

Key Word:
Focus: to concentrate
Synonyms: center, heart, core, nucleus

Explanation:
Many of us like to think that the grass is always greener on the other side. The problem with that way of thinking is that you

will never accomplish what is right in front of you if you can't see it.

Prayer:
Lord, You have put in our hands the things You want us to accomplish for this day. Open our eyes to see it and to do it. Amen

Day 273

Text:
Dd Today: Pr 17 He who covers a transgression seeks love, but he who repeats a matter separates friends. In listening & praying are life, gossip & backbiting, death. ☺

Key Word:
Cover: to place something over or upon, as for protection, concealment, or warmth
Synonyms: cloak, conceal, counterbalance, compensate for

Explanation:
Our words are never as serious as when we are talking about someone else.

Prayer:
Let the words of my mouth and the meditations of my heart be acceptable in Your sight, oh Lord. Amen

Day 274

Text:
Dd Today: Pr 18 A man's stomach shall be satisfied by the fruit of his mouth. By the produce of his lips he shall be filled. What kind of crop are you growing? ☺

Key Word:
Filled: to make full; put as much as can be held into

Synonyms: satisfy, answer, fulfill

Explanation:
A farmer has to sow seed in order to grow a crop, and it is the quality of his seed that determines what kind of crop he will harvest. Good seed, good crops; bad seed, bad crops.

Prayer:
When we speak, let our words sow good seed into the hearer. Amen

Day 275

Text:
Dd Today: Josh 14 Caleb, at 85, came & asked Joshua for the land of the giants as his inheritance. How many of us take the path of least resistance? Go Up! 😊

Key Word:
Resistance: the opposition offered by one thing, force, etc., to another
Synonyms: opposition, obstinacy, defiance, intransigence

Explanation:
I was hunting elk in the Coast Range of Oregon one year and found myself constantly fighting the underbrush to get where I wanted to go. I saw an elk approaching and immediately crouched down. The elk saw me and took off through the brush as if nothing was resisting it. It's not the obstacles that hinder us; it is how we are equipped to handle them that determine our level of resistance.

Prayer:
Lord, help us to put on Your armor each day, so we are better equipped to handle whatever the enemy throws at us. Amen

Day 276

Text:
Dd Today: Pr 20 The spirit of a man is the lamp of the Lord, searching all the inner depths of his heart. Let His light shine in the depth of your closets. ☺

Key Word:
Lamp: a source of intellectual or spiritual light
Synonyms: beacon, light, torch

Explanation:
A room's contents can only be seen if a light is turned on. It is only in our opening up of ourselves to His illumination that we can see what needs cleansing and act on it.

Prayer:
Thank You, Lord, for not shedding Your light on every area of our lives that need adjusting all at one time. Amen

Day 277

Text:
Dd Today: Pr 21 The horse is prepared for the day of battle, but deliverance is of the Lord. When the going gets tough, is what you see, all you see? ☺

Key Word:
Tough: difficult to perform, accomplish, or deal with; hard, trying, or troublesome
Synonyms: firm, hard, durable, inflexible

Explanation:
Sometimes we have to have our eyes opened in order to really see what the true issue is. Linda is very good at opening my eyes to see or look at an issue from a different perspective.

Prayer:
Lord, help not to get tunnel vision and open our eyes to see the real. Amen

Day 278

Text:
Dd Today: Pr 22 A good name is to be chosen over great riches, loving favor rather than silver & gold. You never get a 2nd chance to make a 1st impression. 😊

Key Word:
Chance: an opportune or favorable time; opportunity
Synonyms: prospect, likelihood, opportunity

Explanation:
How many times have you thought to yourself, I wish had that to do over again? A little thought ahead of time would have or could have completely erased that thought.

Prayer:
Thank You, Lord, for being patient enough with us that You give us that second chance. Amen

Day 279

Text:
Dd Today: Josh 15-17 Israel did not drive out all the inhabitants of the land as God had said & they plagued them until this day. Drive ALL enemies out or.. 😊

Key Word:
Plagued: to trouble, annoy, or torment in any manner
Synonyms: harass, vex, harry, hector, fret, worry, badger, irritate, disturb

Explanation:
God wants us to be free of all of our troubles, habits, worries, diseases, etc. We all want to be free, but how willing are we to make the necessary changes to make it happen? Many of us remain enslaved to habits for years, even life times.

Prayer:
Teach us, oh Lord, to walk in Your ways and stick to Your paths. Amen

Day 280

Text:
Dd Today: Jn 4 Jesus said to the woman at the well, give me a drink, but in reality He wanted to give her a drink. Give someone a spirit refreshing drink today. ☺

Key Word:
Refreshing: having the power to restore freshness, vitality, energy
Synonyms: freshen, enliven, reanimate, restore, repair, renovate, renew, retouch

Explanation:
It is so easy to give someone a cool refreshing drink. It might be an encouraging word, flowers, a card, a helping hand, or something as simple as a smile.

Prayer:
Show us creative ways we can give cool refreshing drinks. Amen

Day 281

Text:
Dd Today: Josh 20 The 6 cities of refuge, where one could flee if he committed an unintentional act against another. Today we run to the Lord & we are safe. ☺

Key Word:
Flee: to run away, as from danger or pursuers; take flight
Synonyms: evade, escape, avoid, shun, elude

Explanation:
I have heard many say that becoming a Christian is just an escape, a crutch, a way to avoid reality. Well I say give me that reality and shelter any day.

Prayer:
I run to You Lord and know that You will always accept me no matter where I am at in my life. Amen

Day 282

Text:
Dd Today: Pr 25 Sticks & stones may break my bones, but words will never hurt me, NOT! Even a gentle tongue breaks a bone. Careful little tongue what you say. 😊

Key Word:
Break: to smash, split, or divide into parts violently; reduce to pieces or fragments
Synonyms: fracture, splinter, shiver

Explanation:
I can't tell you how many times people have said to me, "You won't believe what so in so just said, it absolutely devastated me." Our words are so important that a whole portion of the book of Proverbs is dedicated to the tongue. What we say does matter and makes a significant impact.

Prayer:
Let the words of my mouth always reflect You. Amen

Day 283

Text:
Dd Today: Jn 7 If anyone thirsts, let him come to Me & drink. Tap into His well, anticipation & expectation will bring forth refreshing rivers of living water. ☺

Key Word:
Living: active or thriving; vigorous; strong
Synonyms: live, quick, lively, flourishing

Explanation:
Whenever I have come to Him with honest expectation and anticipation, He has never ever failed to deposit in me a stronger desire to move on in Him. That only comes from staying thirsty for His living water. Stay thirsty, my friends!!

Prayer:
Reward our thirsting Lord with Your living water. Amen

Day 284

Text:
Dd Today: Pr 28 Happy is the man who is always reverent- nice, respectful, humble of heart. Remember the old saying, nice guys finish last? I think not!! ☺

Key Word:
Happy: delighted, pleased, or glad, as over a particular thing
Synonyms: joyous, joyful, blithe, cheerful, merry, contented, blissful, satisfied

Explanation:
I had a roommate in college who always use say nice guys finish last. Of course he was referring mostly to the guys who had all the girls and partied most of the time. I'm living proof that nice

guys finish first. I have been married 33 years to a wonderful woman, my kids both serve the Lord with gladness, and my daughter just married an awesome Christian guy.

Prayer:
Thank You, Lord, for honoring those who by the world's standards don't match up, Amen.

Day 285

Text:
Dd Today: Josh 24 Canaan had been given into their hands, Joshua said, choose whom you will serve. As for me & my house, we will serve the Lord! So be it! ☺

Key Word:
Serve: to render assistance; be of use; help, to answer the purpose
Synonyms: attend, aid

Explanation:
You'll notice here serving is a choice and purely voluntary. Serving is honored or respected by the world, but if you notice, not very many practice it on a regular basis. God would that we would cultivate a lifestyle of service.

Prayer:
Make us an instrument of service, Lord. Amen

Day 286

Text:
Dd Today: Jud 1 However, they did not drive out the inhabitants, they did not drive them out... We must have total victory over our enemies. Drive them out! ☺

Key Word:
Total: involving all aspects, elements, participants, resources, etc.; unqualified; all-out
Synonyms: complete, gross, totality, whole

Explanation:
There is no room for part in God's equation. He wants us to be all in.

Prayer:
Help us to be more than conquerors. Amen

Day 287

Text:
Dd Today: Pr 30 Every word of God is pure; He is a shield to those who put their trust in Him. Put your hand in His; just put your hand in His. ☺

Key Word:
Shield: a broad piece of armor, varying widely in form and size, carried apart from the body, usually on the left arm, as a defense against swords, lances, arrows, etc.
Synonyms: screen, protect, secure, shelter, protector

Explanation:
When we were pastors, I remember a number of obvious attacks of the enemy, i.e. well going dry, breakdown of appliances, flat tires, etc. The best thing about these is we knew that because of them we were in the right place making an impact. He was always faithful to supply our needs from water to finances.

Prayer:
In faithfulness we put our trust in You. Amen

Day 288

Text:
Dd Today: Jn 10 Jesus is the door & the good shepherd, when the shepherd speaks the sheep hear & follow. When He speaks do we hear & follow? ☺

Key Word:
Speaks: to communicate, signify, or disclose by any means; convey significance
Synonyms: pronounce, articulate, say, disclose

Explanation:
I think the key here is found in what James said, that we need to not only be hearers of the Word, but more importantly, to be doers.

Prayer:
Increase our sensitivity, Lord, in both hearing and carrying out what we hear. Amen

Day 289

Text:
Dd Today: Josh 2 Joshua died & all his generation w/him. Another generation arose who did not know the Lord. We are to make sure those that follow, know Him. ☺

Key Word:
Know: to perceive or understand as fact or truth; to apprehend clearly and with certainty
Synonyms: comprehend, understand

Explanation:
It is not enough for you to live for Him, but we have been saddled with the joy of seeing that the next generation also

follows Him. We have had the joy of seeing our kids live for Him with impact.

Prayer:
Lord, lift our vision higher so that the next generation will continue in You. Amen

Day 290

Text:
Dd Today: Jn 11 Jesus wept over His friend Lazarus because He loved him. The wonderful mystery is, He loves us with that same compassion. Love Him back!! 😊

Key Word:
Love: a feeling of warm personal attachment or deep affection, as for a parent, child, or friend
Synonyms: tenderness, fondness, predilection, warmth, passion, adoration

Explanation:
There is nothing comparable to the feeling when I came to the realization that God truly loves me and laid down His life for me. When I came to know Him, I was overwhelmed with His love and wanted to return that love.

Prayer:
Lord, thank You for first loving us enough to die for us. Amen

Day 291

Text:
Dd Today: Jn 13 Jesus was no respecter of persons, He even washed Judas' feet, He loved him, knowing what he was about to do. We may know, but would we do it? 😊

Key Word:
Respect: esteem for or a sense of the worth or excellence of a person, a personal quality or ability, or something considered as a manifestation of a personal quality or ability
Synonyms: regard, esteem, estimation

Explanation:
Knowing what He knew and doing what He did was an example that had far-reaching consequences among the disciples. I would have a very hard time doing what He did.

Prayer:
It may be hard, but teach us to do as You do. Amen

Day 292

Text:
Dd Today: Jn 14 He who believes in Me, the works that I do he will do also & greater works he will do. If you ask anything in my name, I will do it. Believe, ask! ☺

Key Word:
Ask: to put a question to; inquire of
Synonyms: question, inquire, entreat

Explanation:
I find it hard to believe that we would be able to do greater works than He did. That being said, I have seen Him heal individuals through me and after reading the book of Acts, Ask!

Prayer:
Lord, help our unbelief. Amen

Day 293

Text:
Dd Today: Jud 6 The Angel put out His staff & fire came out of the rock & consumed the sacrifice. Gideon perceived he was an Angel, duh! Obvious? Not always. ☺

Key Word:
Perceived: to become aware of directly through any of the senses, especially sight or hearing
Synonyms: note, discover, observe, descry, distinguish

Explanation:
There are many occasions in which God takes action, and we don't have a clue that He was even involved. Sometimes we even attribute them to Satan. I think He would like us to become a bit more sensitive.

Prayer:
Lord, increase our sensitivity to You and Your workings. Amen

Day 294

Text:
Dd Today: Jn 15 Every branch that bears fruit He prunes that it may bear more fruit. Fruit bearers beware, Master pruner on the job. ☺

Key Word:
Prunes: to cut or lop superfluous or undesired twigs, branches, or roots from; trim
Synonyms: clip, knock off, pare, exclude, cut back, snip, shave

Explanation:
If you're not into pruning, don't serve Him. He is the master pruner and isn't satisfied with the status quo.

Prayer:
Clip, knock off, pare, cut back, whatever it is You deem unnecessary. Amen

Day 295

Text:
Dd Today: Jud 8 Gideon, after saving Israel, made an ephod of gold & they worshipped it. Never take for granted the Lord's work. It will be a snare to you. ☺

Key Word:
take for granted: to underestimate the value of
Synonyms: accept blindly, underestimate

Explanation:
Sometimes our strengths can be a double weakness. In this case, success went to their head.

Prayer:
Help us to remain mindful that our success is only by Your hand. Amen

Day 296

Text:
Dd Today: Jn 21 Jesus told them to cast their net again, their catch was overwhelming yet their nets held. When He speaks to us, our nets will be full & hold. ☺

Key Word:
Hold: to remain fast; adhere; cling
Synonyms: persist, last, endure, stick

Explanation:
The disciples may have questioned whether they should cast their nets in a second time, but the catch and security of their nets convinced them never to doubt acting on His word.

Prayer:
When You speak, open our ears to hear. Amen

Day 297

Text:
Dd Today: Pr 19 What is desired in a man is kindness. Let's kill them with kindness and win them with goodness. ☺

Key Word:
Desired: deemed correct or proper; selected; required
Synonyms: coveted, in demand, sought after, craved

Explanation:
There are very few people who won't respond to kindness and goodness. He was good to us; shouldn't we reflect that to others? Love covers their sins, and kindness and goodness win them over.

Prayer:
Thank You for being the ultimate example to us. We don't deserve it. Amen

Day 298

Text:
Dd Today: Acts 1 These all continued with one accord... unity & harmony always gets His attention. ☺

Key Word:
Continued: lasting or enduring without interruption
Synonyms: endure, persist, persevere, last, remain

Explanation:
God was concerned when the people got together and began to build the Tower of Babel because He knew what unity and harmony could do. When the disciples did as He asked and continued in one accord, He rewarded them with the H.S. and turned the world upside down.

Prayer:
Lord, help us to lay aside our differences to see Your kingdom advanced. Amen

Day 299

Text:
Dd Today: Jud 16 Samson did not know that the Lord had departed from him. We can lose our sensitivity to His presence & not realize our full potential in Him. ☺

Key Word:
Departed: to go away; leave
Synonyms: depart, retire, retreat, withdraw

Explanation:
In the OT the HS would descend and withdraw after a deed was accomplished. In Samson's case, this happened multiple times, and he became unaware that the Spirit had departed, leaving him like any other man. In the NT the Spirit descended and remained, thus is always with us. However, we can become like Samson in that we lose our sensitivity to His presence.

Prayer:
Lord, help us to be like David in requesting that You take not Your HS from us. Amen

Day 300

Text:
Dd Today: Pr 8 That I may cause those who love me to inherit wealth, that I may fill their treasuries. Love wisdom & it will only do you good all of your days. ☺

Key Word:
Inherit: to receive as one's portion; come into possession of
Synonyms: come into, get, receive

Explanation:
Solomon was adamant that the only thing he wanted from the Lord was wisdom, and look what He did for him. My first and foremost desire is for Him to give me wisdom and all these other things will be added to me.

Prayer:
Give us wisdom above all else, Lord. Amen

Day 301

Text:
Dd Today: Pr 9 What the Lord has put in your hand to do, do it with all your might. Constantly wishing you were somewhere else only distracts from the now. ☺

Key Word:
Distracts: To cause to turn away from the original focus of attention or interest; divert
Synonyms: bewilder, agitate, pain, torment, distress

Explanation:
Have you ever been in the middle of a task and had the thought, I'd really rather be somewhere other than where I am doing something else? Well, I have, a million times, and I have to

reign in those thoughts and make sure the task at hand is not only done, but done well.

Prayer:
Lord, we have all had these times, but help us to focus on the task at hand and do it with all our might. Amen

Day 302

Text:
Dd Today: Pr 11 The Lord delights in the ways of the blameless. Remember He delights in our blamelessness & does not expect us to be perfect. ☺

Key Word:
Blameless: free from or not deserving blame; guiltless
Synonyms: irreproachable, harmless, guiltless, inculpable

Explanation:
Back in the Garden there was a lot of blaming going on, but the Lord wants us to be above all that. He knows we're not perfect, thus the expectation of us being blameless. We will make mistakes, and He accepts us right where we are.

Prayer:
Lord, thank You for accepting us right where we are without reservation. Amen

Day 303

Text:
Dd Today: Pr 13 He who walks with wise men will be wise, but the companion of fools will be destroyed. You become like who you hang with. Who do you hang with? ☺

Key Word:
Hang: to consort or appear in public with, to loiter in public places

Synonyms: fraternize, spend time with, suspend

Explanation:
I think virtually everyone is aware that whoever you spend the most time with, you will tend to be like that person. Someone once said, you are the sum of the five people closest to you.

Prayer:
Lord, help us to accountable and not an account of our closest friends. Amen

Day 304

Text:
Dd Today: Pr 20 Plans are established by counsel, by wise counsel wage war. Always hit the floor before taking your first step. ☺

Key Word:
Wage: to carry on (a battle, war, conflict, argument, etc.
Synonyms: undertake, prosecute, contend, struggle

Explanation:
My son has made a habit of calling me before he makes a major decision. Sometimes I don't even have to give him my opinion, it is simply him talking it through and hearing his own words that give him the advice he needed. Still, other times I give him my advice. The fact that he asks at all is the healthy part.

Prayer:
There is more to our decisions than just what we think. Help us Lord to always look to You first and others before making them. Amen

Day 305

Text:
Dd Today: Heb 11 Looking beyond our circumstances, let's grab onto that substance we hope for, hold it tight & evidence through hope, will begin to appear. 😊

Key Word:
Beyond: outside the understanding, limits, or reach of; past
Synonyms: over, outside, after, remote, ahead, besides

Explanation:
As for me, I have the most common ability to hardly ever look beyond what is in front of me, which is most unfortunate. My wife, on the other hand, almost always looks past what is and can see what could be. The one thing I have discovered is that this is a learned behavior and we non-seers can become seers.

Prayer:
Lord, continue to challenge us to look beyond what is to the what could be. Amen

Day 306

Text:
Dd Today: Acts 17 He is not far from each of us, for in Him we live, move & have our being. Outside of the Lord there is no you. Our very identity is in Him. 😊

Key Word:
Identity: condition or character as to who a person or what a thing is
Synonyms: individuality, personality, distinctiveness, uniqueness

Explanation:
I think we must come to the realization that He created this whole thing to start with, and should He decided to discontinue

the program, we would all be up a creek without a paddle. My relationship to Him is the most important thing there is.

Prayer:
Show us, Lord, and help us all to come to the realization that You are You. Amen

Day 307

Text:
Dd Today: 1 Sam 7 Samuel had Israel put away their idols & entreat God for favor against the Phillistines. Put away distractions & hearing is much clearer. ☺

Key Word:
Clearer: easily seen; sharply defined, distinctly perceptible to the ear; easily heard
Synonyms: unimpeded, unobstructed, unhampered, unencumbered

Explanation:
I can remember doing a home group message on prayer, and my main illustration was myself kneeling and allowing everyone, every action to keep me from concentrating on prayer. So often we allow our own thoughts to keep us from the very thing we are trying to accomplish.

Prayer:
Focus, focus, focus! Keep us from the those things that so easily distract. Amen

Day 308

Text:
Dd Today: 1 Sam 8 Samuel warned the people of the consequences of having a king, yet the people still rejected God. Seeking your own will only brings trouble. ☺

Key Word:
Consequences: an act or instance of following something as an effect, result, or outcome
Synonyms: outcome, issue, upshot, sequel

Explanation:
I like the word sequel here because so many times we act totally shocked by the outcome of a comment or action that we didwhen in reality it was only the natural sequel to our previous sequence of comments or actions.

Prayer:
Somehow keep us mindful or our mouths and actions. Amen

Day 309

Text:
Dd Today: Pr 25 It is the glory of God to hide a matter, the glory of kings is to search it out. We feel the need to find out, He already knows. 😊

Key Word:
Already: by this or that time; previously; prior to or at some specified or implied time
Synonyms: heretofore, formerly, earlier, previously

Explanation:
I once asked a great Biblical scholar how long he had been studying and searching the Bible. He looked at me with a most genuine of smiles and said, "I can't remember not studying it." He went on to say that it is our responsibility to search out the matter, but it is God's to bring illumination as to what it really means.

Prayer:
Lord, never let the hunger for knowledge run dry and always feed us with Your wisdom as to what to do with it. Amen

Day 310

Text:
Dd Today: Acts 20 Paul, knowing the course before him, pressed on without regret. If we knew our course, looking back & forward, what would our response be? ☺

Key Word:
Pressed: to act upon with steadily applied weight or force
Synonyms: induce, persuade, beg, implore

Explanation:
Many of us already know what our course should be. The trouble is we are willing to endure what it will take to get us there. We take the path of least resistance.

Prayer:
Show us our path and help us to realize that with You our resolve to accomplish it is right before us. Amen

Day 311

Text:
Dd Today: 1 Sam 10 The Spirit of the Lord will come upon you & you will be turned into another man. His Spirit will change us, only if we will let Him. ☺

Key Word:
Another: different; distinct; of a different period, place, or kind
Synonyms: more, other, added, different, additional

Explanation:
The funny thing about God is that He isn't satisfied for us to remain the same. He is infinitely more interested in our character than our comfort.

Prayer:
Lord, make us uncomfortable to point of change. Amen

Day 312

Text:
Dd Today: Pr 28 He who covers his sins will not prosper. But whoever confesses & forsakes them will have mercy. Confession opens, forsaking closes the chapter. ☺

Key Word:
Confess: to acknowledge or avow (a fault, misdeed, weakness, etc.) by way of revelation
Synonyms: admit, unload, come out, declare

Explanation:
I think we tend to keep things to ourselves and say we have taken care of them rather than openly admit, come out, acknowledge that we have a weakness. God would have us open up with our mouth admitting our weaknesses, therefore holding ourselves accountable.

Prayer:
Lord, help us to come out of the secret place and face ourselves. Amen

Day 313

Text:
Dd Today: Pr 29 The fear of man brings a snare, whoever trusts in the Lord shall be safe. Fear-False Evidence 'Appearing' Real, the Lord very simply 'IS'! ☺

Key Word:
Fear: a distressing emotion aroused by impending danger, evil, pain, etc., whether the threat is real or imagined; the feeling or condition of being afraid

Synonyms: apprehension, consternation, dismay, terror, fright, panic, horror, trepidation

Explanation:
Once we understand that fear never comes from God but from the devil, then we begin the journey of putting it under our feet, once and for all.

Prayer:
Thanks, Lord, for being a God of peace and love and for giving ultimate victory over the evil one. Amen

Day 314

Text:
Dd Today: 1 Sam 13 Saul assumed it was ok to perform the sacrifice since Samuel wasn't there yet. We all know what assuming does, clear it with Him first. 😊

Key Word:
Assume: to take for granted or without proof; suppose; postulate; posit
Synonyms: presuppose, pretend

Explanation:
I don't think I have ever assumed or taken for granted anything in my life, NOT!! We all have made assumptions over the years that have eventually come back to haunt us. He would like to help us eliminate the consequences thereof. Consult Him first, and you will.

Prayer:
Lord, help us to create a habit of always looking to You first. Amen

Day 315

Text:
Dd Today: 1 Sam 15 Saul disobeyed the Lord & did not utterly destroy the Amalekites, keeping some for sacrifice. Sam nailed him, obedience is better than sacrifice. ☺

Key Word:
Obedience: the act or practice of obeying; dutiful or submissive compliance
Synonyms: submission, subservience, deference

Explanation:
I remember standing in a field of potatoes telling myself I would not hoe the weeds because I wanted to be somewhere else. I don't know how long I stood there, but it didn't matter. I could have been done with the weeds and off doing what I wanted if I had just been obedient in the first place. Disobedience never pays!!

Prayer:
I choose to obey Your every word without hesitation. Amen

Day 316

Text:
Dd Today: 1 Sam 16 The Lord does not see as man sees, a man looks on the outward appearance, the Lord looks at the heart. Lord, open our eyes as Yours. ☺

Key Word:
Outward: pertaining to or being what is seen or apparent, as distinguished from the underlying nature, facts, etc.; pertaining to surface qualities only; superficial
Synonyms: ostensible, exterior, perceptible, outer, apparent

Explanation:
We have all found ourselves leaning more towards certain individuals because of what they are wearing or how they look, and then, after getting to know them a bit, finding out they are totally messed up inside. When the Lord cleans up the inside, the outside isn't long to follow.

Prayer:
Lord, help us to see with Your eyes and not rely on our own senses. Amen

Day 317

Text:
Dd Today: 1 Sam 17 David served the living God, Goliath the idols of the Phillistines. Be careful to know who you serve, one brings victory, the other????. ☺

Key Word:
Careful: attentive to potential danger, error, or harm; cautious
Synonyms: watchful, guarded, chary, circumspect, careful, cautious, discreet, wary

Explanation:
When I was younger, I would go to work wherever I could find a job, but it didn't take me long to realize that who I worked for was oftentimes very beneficial to what I was trying to accomplish. It wasn't what I knew, it was who I knew.

Prayer:
Lord, lead us to right relationships. Amen

Day 318

Text:
Dd Today: Pr 3 Trust in the Lord w/some of your heart... in most of your ways acknowledge Him...no, in ALL your ways, then, He shall direct your paths. 😊

Key Word:
Some: being a portion or an unspecified number or quantity of a whole or group
Synonyms: more or less, approximately, several

Explanation:
Back when I was in sports, it was the guys who gave it all who generally remained healthy and got to play almost all the time. Those who gave it less than 100% were always on the outside looking in.

Prayer:
Lord, we give You all of us. Amen

Day 319

Text:
Dd Today: Pr 4 Keep your mind, will & emotions with all diligence, for out of them come the issues of life. Do you have ACD? Attitude Checks Daily. 😊

Key Word:
Diligence: constant and earnest effort to accomplish what is undertaken; persistent exertion of body or mind
Synonyms: heed, carefulness, keenness, attentiveness, industriousness, pertinacity, intensity

Explanation:
It wasn't always easy to listen to what the coach wanted us to do, but when we did, we usually got the job done.

Prayer:
Lord, help us to be attentive to Your direction, and we'll accomplish a whole lot more. Amen

Day 320

Text:
Dd Today: Rom 3 Jesus stepped out of eternity w/all its majesty & glory, gave it all up for us. Let's step out of our everyday & give it up for Him. 😊

Key Word:
Step out: to withdraw; quit
Synonyms: exit, interrupt, change direction, risk

Explanation:
I am an ordered person and like things to be that way; however, I can think of a few times when I got outside my comfort zone and took a risk. That's what we need to do more often, and it will bring a new perspective on life.

Prayer:
Lord, help us to see outside the box like you do. Amen

Day 321

Text:
Dd Today: Rom 4 Abraham believed God who calls those things which do not exist as though they did. We all need an Abe experience, seeing beyond the now. 😊

Key Word:
Beyond: outside the understanding, limits, or reach of; past
Synonyms: remote, ahead, over, farther, past, yonder

Explanation:
In every game, there is a game within the game that is always taking place. When you are watching any sporting event and can see beyond the surface of what is going down, it makes the game that much more interesting. God would like us to see beyond the surface of our lives and grasp that portion of life going on over and past what we see.

Prayer:
There is a place that allows us to see beyond the nasty now and now. Lord, take us there. Amen

Day 322

Text:
Dd Today: 1 Sam 23 Every time David sought the Lord before making a decision, He was faithful to answer him. How much more should we before our decisions? ☺

Key Word:
Sought: to ask for; request
Synonyms: pursue, follow

Explanation:
Most everyone knows it's best to sleep on every decision, but the key to sleeping on it lies in who we consult with during that sleeping time.

Prayer:
Lord, show us Your faithfulness in the sleeping time. Amen

Day 323

Text:
Dd Today: Pr 9 Wisdom has built her house..the fear of the Lord is the beginning of wisdom. If true, why do we exhaust OUR devices before the Lord's? ☺

Key Word:
Exhaust: to use up or consume completely; expend the whole of
Synonyms: eat up, overdo, conk out, dissipate, dry, weary, draw

Explanation:
I can't tell you the number of times I have worked and worked and worked to solve a random issue or problem, and after exhausting all my resources that I can muster, out of extreme frustration and sometimes anger, I look up and say, "It's Your turn." Then I can almost hear Him laughing, yet the answer comes in a very short moment.

Prayer:
Lord, help us to minimize our efforts and maximize Yours. Amen

Day 324

Text:
Dd Today: Rom 5 Tribulation produces perseverance, perseverance character, character hope. Remember, God is more interested in our character than our comfort. 😊

Key Word:
Character: moral or ethical quality
Synonyms: moral qualities, ethical standards, principles, moral excellence

Explanation:
There are so many times over the years that I have been put into positions or circumstances or situations that only appeared awkward and sometimes meaningless at the time, but looking back, it was God shaping and molding my character, using those influences as part of the process.

Prayer:
God, help us to be sensitive to Your character building moments. Amen

Day 325

Text:
Dd Today: Rom 5 We will scarcely die for a good man let alone an enemy. Yet He died for us in spite of our selves. What your excuse, yeah but, but what? ☺

Key Word:
Excuse: an explanation offered to justify or obtain forgiveness
Synonyms: rationalize, vindicate, plea, jive

Explanation:
We really have no excuse when it comes to what Jesus did for us. Ours is to respond.

Prayer:
Help us to come to You with no pretense or excuses. Amen

Day 326

Text:
Dd Today: Rom 5 For as by one man's disobedience many were made sinners, so also by one Man's obedience many will be made righteous. Obedience? Oh my! OK! ☺

Key Word:
Disobedience: lack of obedience or refusal to comply; disregard or transgression
Synonyms: recalcitrance, nonobservance, noncompliance, infringement, violation

Explanation:
Adam made his decision, and we all paid for it. Jesus made His decision and paid for us. What's your decision: obedience or disobedience?

Prayer:
I thank You that Your Son made His decision and that You also offered us a decision. Amen

Day 327

Text:
Dd Today: 1 Sam 24 David refused to stretch out his hand against Saul, the Lord's anointed. Regardless, it is our duty to honor those over us. Ouch!! Ok Lord! ☺

Key Word:
Honor: high respect, as for worth, merit, or rank
Synonyms: admire, adoration, celebrate, respect

Explanation:
In America we have the privilege to select those who rule over us, and in many ways, God puts those in position for a reason. Regardless of whether or not our candidate was elected, it is still our responsibility to give honor and respect to that office and it is also our responsibility to pray for them. We can disagree, but ultimately God is in control.

Prayer:
Lord, give us a heart for those who rule over us. Amen

Day 328

Text:
Dd Today: Rom 8 We know that all things work together for good to those who love God, to those who are the called according to His purpose. Do we really? ☺

Key Word:
Know: to perceive or understand as fact or truth; to apprehend clearly and with certainty
Synonyms: differentiate, discriminate, identify, understand, recognize

Explanation:
I think, if we all were to look at our lives, there would be so many things we could identify that at first seemed negative or even horrible, yet we saw God turn those things into something we could never have imagined possible, something, only He could accomplish.

Prayer:
There are so many things, Lord, to be thankful for, and we simply Thank You. Amen

Day 329

Text:
Dd Today: Rom 9 Does not the potter have power over the clay, from the same lump to make one vessel for honor, another for dishonor? Choose your vessel well. ☺

Key Word:
Vessel: a person regarded as a holder or receiver of something
Synonyms: basin, boat, utensil, craft

Explanation:
The greatest aspect of this story is God gave us the ability to choose the type of vessel we want to be. It is our everyday choices that mold our vessel into what it is, and occasionally, God chooses to allow our vessels to be broken. Thankfully, He has the ability to remake our vessel as well.

Prayer:
Lord, make us an instrument in Your hand. Amen

Day 330

Text:
Dd Today: Pr 14 He who is slow to wrath has great understanding, but he who is impulsive exalts folly. We may lose a few skirmishes, but Self Control wins wars. ☺

Key Word:
Slow: taking or requiring a comparatively long time for completion
Synonyms: unhurried, slow, deliberate, gradual, leisurely

Explanation:
This is the part of my character in which God and I have had some moments. I may not seem like an angry man, but let's just say I have had my struggles over the years. I have lost my share of skirmishes, but the good thing is that I'm winning the war with His help.

Prayer:
Lord, I thank You for Your faithfulness over the years. You never gave up, and consequently, I didn't either. Thanks, Amen

Day 331

Text:
Dd Today: Rom 10 For w/the heart one believes unto righteousness & w/the mouth confession is made unto salvation. Listen & you will know what one believes. ☺

Key Word:
Believe: to be persuaded of the truth or existence of
Synonyms: confident, accredit, presume, conclude

Explanation:
Have a conversation with a person who has just been through a crisis, and you will find out very quickly what that person actually believes. They may profess a lot of things, but when

the rubber hits the road, their true beliefs will come shining or vice versa through.

Prayer:
Lord, when the heat is turned up, let us always be true to You. Amen

Day 332

Text:
Dd Today: 1 Sam 30 All were distressed because their families had been taken, but David 'strengthened himself in the Lord'. Sometimes we just have to stand. ☺

Key Word:
Strengthened: to make stronger; give strength to
Synonyms: buttress, reinforce, fortify, support

Explanation:
I know I have had many opportunities not to stand. The circumstances pointed in one direction, and it would have been much easier to go with the flow, but somehow that didn't seem like the right thing to do. So you pull yourself up by your bootstraps, look up to whence commeth your help, and stand.

Prayer:
Thank You, Lord, for men like David, examples we can relate to and follow. Amen

Day 333

Text:
Dd Today: Rom 12 Do not be conformed to this world, but be transformed by the renewing of your mind. How is the transformation coming along? Forward or...? ☺

Key Word:
Transform: to change in condition, nature, or character; convert
Synonyms: transfigure, convert

Explanation:
Sometimes we just have to let go and let God as cliché as that sounds.

Prayer:
Help us to let go of all that so easily holds us back. Amen

Day 334

Text:
Dd Today: Rom 12 Let love be without hypocrisy. Abhor what is evil. Cling to what is good. What Paul is saying here, if you are a Christian, act like one! 😊

Key Word:
Hypocrisy: a pretense of having a virtuous character, moral or religious beliefs or principles, etc., that one does not really possess
Synonyms: mockery, deception, fraud, quackery, casuistry

Explanation:
I think everyone can identify with this one because we've all run into that person who espouses to be a Christian, but their actions scream something else. If you are one, be one!! If you say you are a Christian, be one!!

Prayer:
Lord, give us the plumb line of Amos and help us stick to it. Amen

Day 335

Text:
Dd Today: Rom 12 Be of the same mind toward one another & assoc w/the humble. Do not be wise in your own opinion. Ah, the fundamentals of our faith, refreshing. ☺

Key Word:
Same: similar in kind, quality, quantity, or degree
Synonyms: corresponding, interchangeable, equal

Explanation:
This is all about hearing and doing, functioning and responding together. The church in the book of Acts all worked together in one accord, which brought the results they experienced.

Prayer:
Lord, release Your Spirit and anointing to draw us together as one. Amen

Day 336

Text:
Dd Today: Pr 21 There are many plans in a man's heart, nevertheless the LORD's counsel that will stand. Make sure the Lord is in it, before going forward. ☺

Key Word:
Stand: to remain firm or steadfast, as in a cause
Synonyms: abide, support, hold, steadfast

Explanation:
Hopefully we have all had plans of one sort or another; the critical element we tend to leave out is the Lord. What's His opinion? It's the only one that really counts anyhow.

Prayer:
Lord, we only want to proceed with Your blessing. Amen

Day 337

Text:
Dd Today: Pr 20 Avoiding a fight is a mark of honor; only fools insist on quarreling. Self Control is more than what we see on a page. Practice makes perfect. 😊

Key Word:
Avoid: to keep away from; keep clear of; shun
Synonyms: elude, escape

Explanation:
When we first got married, we set up rules of engagement when it came to fighting or heated fellowship as we like to call it. I didn't mean to do ... always turned into did you mean not to do it. The key is using enough self-control to mean not to do it.

Prayer:
Lord, help us to think in terms of meaning not to do it. Amen

Day 338

Text:
Dd Today: Rom 15 Now may the God of hope fill you w/ all joy & peace in believing, that you may abound in hope by the power of the H S. There is always hope. 😊

Key Word:
Hope: to believe, desire, or trust
Synonyms: expectancy, longing

Explanation:
With God there is always hope. When we come to the place where we can wrap our head and our heart around that fact, we will see that He is good, and good things are just around the corner.

Prayer:
Thank You, Lord, for never ever leaving us or forsaking us. Amen

Day 339

Text:
Dd Today: Rom 16 I want you to be wise in what is good, and simple concerning evil. And the God of peace will crush Satan under your feet shortly. Crushed is good! ☺

Key Word:
Crush: to destroy, subdue, or suppress utterly
Synonyms: pulverize, powder, mash, crumble, break

Explanation:
I've known people who have studied evil, and the unfortunate thing is that they tended to become like what they were focused on. Those who studied the good and positive tended to be good and positive. Which would you prefer?

Prayer:
Lord, You created us in Your image. Keep our focus on You and not on the evil one. Amen

Day 340

Text:
Dd Today: 2 Sam 5 David said, The LORD has broken through my enemies before me, like a breakthrough of water. Deliverance came, let the waves crush our enemy. ☺

Key Word:
Breakthrough: a military movement or advance all the way through andbeyond an enemy's front-line defense
Synonyms: increase, improvement, progress, quantum leap

Explanation:
There are so many scriptures regarding the Lord conquering the enemy and overcoming the enemy. We are to be overcomers. If we will just trust Him, I have seen so many times that the Lord has come through on our behalf. Lean on Him.

Prayer:
Show us Your power, Lord. Amen

Day 341

Text:
Dd Today: Pr 24 Through wisdom a house is built and by understanding it is established. In listening we hear, in seeing we understand. Open our eyes & ears. 😊

Key Word:
Open: to clear (a passage, channel, etc.) of obstructions
Synonyms: see, break out

Explanation:
When asking Him to open our eyes and ears, we want to see and to hear from His perspective as best we can. We all have various filters we see and hear through, but the idea here is to put aside the filtration process.

Prayer:
Help us to put aside the inherent filters we see and hear through. Amen

Day 342

Text:
Dd Today: 1 Cor 6 All things are lawful for me, but I will not be brought under the power of any. Who rules us, the Creator or the created? 😊

Key Word:
Creator: a person or thing that creates
Synonyms: parent, maker, father, producer, sire

Explanation:
The key here is examining ourselves and our lives to determine just who is in control. Do the things around us have more influence than the one who created the things around us?

Prayer:
Help us, Lord, not to lose focus of who You really are. Amen

Day 343

Text:
Dd Today: 2 Sam 11 David, as great a man as he was in the sight of the Lord, displeased Him. We all fall short. Thank God, His arm is long & grace sufficient. 😊

Key Word:
Displeased: to incur the dissatisfaction, dislike, or disapproval of; offend; annoy
Synonyms: disappointed, annoyed, angry, dissatisfied

Explanation:
The one thing David understood above all else is God's grace. We all could use a transfusion from David's life, injecting large doses of grace at every turn.

Prayer:
Help us, Lord, to come to a full realization of Your grace and how all encompassing it is. Amen

Day 344

Text:
Dd Today: Pr 28 He who covers his sins will not prosper, But whoever confesses and forsakes them will have mercy. David did both & received mercy. Who are we? 😊

Key Word:
Receive: to take into one's possession (something offered or delivered)
Synonyms: admit, entertain, welcome

Explanation:
We have become a society adept at covering up things, and unfortunately, our examples in positions of authority have failed us miserably. All the more reason to turn to the Lord and His word, which will bring sanity into an otherwise very confusing world.

Prayer:
Show us how to stop what we are doing so as to stop what we have been getting. Amen

Day 345

Text:
Dd Today: 2 Sam 12 David's response to the word of the Lord from Nathan was to humble himself, then get up. When the Lord comes to us do we hold on or let go? 😊

Key Word:
Response: an answer or reply, as in words or in some action
Synonyms: reply, rejoinder, acknowledgment

Explanation:
David could have argued with Nathan over the details and made many excuses as to why he did what he did, but he did none of the above. His total response was one of accepting or taking responsibility for what he had done and then, humbling himself before God, begging forgiveness. Excuses are easy, but consequences are hard.

Prayer:
Lord, help us to take responsibility for our actions and come humbly before You. Amen

Day 346

Text:
Dd Today: Pr 29 A fool vents all his feelings, But a wise man holds them back. How many times have you felt like blasting someone, but didn't, oh! you did? 😊

Key Word:
Vents: to give free play or expression to (an emotion, passion, etc.)
Synonyms: exit, mouth, opening, outlet, pipe

Explanation:
We have all seen knee-jerk reactions where someone simply couldn't control themselves and unleashed a very ungodly attack. The best place to see this is at a little league baseball game. I have done it, and I have also had to go back and apologize for my actions. Controlling yourself causes a whole lot less embarrassment.

Prayer:
Lord, give us opportunity to hone our skill at self control. Amen

Day 347

Text:
Dd Today: 1 Cor 9 I have made myself a servant to all, that I might win the more. Many will follow as we improve our serve. ☺

Key Word:
Serve: to render assistance; be of use; help
Synonyms: wait on, attend, nurse, aid, succor

Explanation:
I think we would all agree that we have the most respect for those who serve in one way or another. The one who saves someone's life in a car accident or plane crash, helps distribute food at a food bank, the teacher who went out of their way to make sure you understood the question. Being a servant sometimes takes great effort, other times is effortless, but nevertheless it's always what the Lord Jesus Christ wanted us to get.

Prayer:
Help us get it. Amen

Day 348

Text:
Dd Today: 1 Cor 9 We all run the race, but not all strategically for it is in strategy & planning which keep our focus & example true w/out disqualification. ☺

Key Word:
Strategy: a plan, method, or series of maneuvers or stratagems forobtaining a specific goal or result
Synonyms: setup, project, plan, layout, tactics

Explanation:
As in any sport, it takes preparation, practice and planning to be able to participate at a high level. It is no different in the daily race we run as Paul put it here. The larger than life object of all the preparation, practice and planning is not to avoid disqualification, but to win.

Prayer:
Show us Your strategy for our race. Amen

Day 349

Text:
Dd Today: 1 Cor 8 In taking our liberty we think that there is nothing to worry about. Take care, lest in stumbling we cause others to stumble. ☺

Key Word:
Stumble: to strike the foot against something, as in walking or running, so as to stagger or fall; trip
Synonyms: muddle, falter, fudge, waver, slip up

Explanation:
Paul also says that taking an occasion for the flesh, i.e. having a drink with an alcoholic, and causing them to stumble is something we need to make sure we are aware of and avoid if at all possible.

Prayer:
Lord, help us to see those situations coming and avoid them. Amen

Day 350

Text:
Dd Today: 1 Cor 11 Imitate me, just as I also imitate Christ. Paul makes this bold statement, in many ways we all could do the same, ENJOY your life in Christ! ☺

Key Word:
Imitate: to follow or endeavor to follow as a model or example
Synonyms: copy, duplicate, reproduce

Explanation:
I think it's pretty clear here that Paul wants us all to walk in such a way that anyone coming into contact with us would have a desire well up within them to walk as we walk.

Prayer:
Lord, help us to walk in the manner of a role model. Amen

Day 351

Text:
Dd Today: Pr 1 Whoever listens to Me will dwell safely, And will be secure, without fear of evil. Lord, dig our ears deep that we would always hear You. ☺

Key Word:
Listen: to give attention with the ear; attend closely for the purpose of hearing; give ear
Synonyms: hear, receive, attend

Explanation:
Without sensitivity and an ear to hear, we would never have done half the things or experienced life the way we have. The impact we have had was only due to our being open and listening for His direction. It came in many different forms: His word, an audible voice, leaders, friends, prophets, strangers, etc.

Prayer:
Lord, keep us in that place where sensitivity dwells. Amen

Day 352

Text:
Dd Today: 1Cor13 When I was a child, I spoke, understood & thought as a child; but as a man, I put away childish things. We are to be like them not as them. 😊

Key Word:
Childish: puerile; weak; silly
Synonyms: foolish, babyish, infantine, puerile

Explanation:
As we approach the things of God, He would want us to come as a child, i.e. pure, fresh, innocent, and accepting. He never wants us to lose those traits. He does, however, want us to grow up in our faith, much like we do in life. We take on responsibility and mature in our ability to make decisions.

Prayer:
Lord, help us to always hold onto that child within us. Amen

Day 353

Text:
Dd Today: Pr 4 Do not turn to the right or the left; Remove your foot from evil. Personal responsibility, God will not do it for you. 😊

Key Word:
Remove: to move from a place or position; take away or off
Synonyms: dislodge, displace, transport

Explanation:
There is never any substitute for taking personal responsibility. I know what first prompted me to write this book was taking personal control and being responsible for my family. And that is what I'm hoping my book will do for its readers.

Prayer:
Lord, do not let us shirk our responsibility as you did with me. Amen

Day 354

Text:
Dd Today: 1 Cor 15 Paul states the 1st is the natural & then comes the spiritual. Some of us are so heavenly minded we are of no earthly good. ☺

Key Word:
Natural: having a real or physical existence, as opposed to one that is spiritual, intellectual, fictitious, etc
Synonyms: spontaneous, unaffected, genuine

Explanation:
I think when it comes to living life, we have to stop and take into consideration the natural things we encounter every day. Our physical environment and those things which have a definite influence on what we do and say. Then we can begin to overlay the spiritual principles that govern our physical existence and apply them practically to our circumstances.

Prayer:
Lord, help us to be practically minded and spiritually applicable. Amen

Day 355

Text:
Dd Today: Pr 8 Solomon asked for wisdom, My fruit is better than gold, yes, than fine gold, And my revenue than choice silver. It's ours for the asking. ☺

Key Word:
Ask: to make a request
Synonyms: question, beseech, entreat

Explanation:
I really think we can learn volumes from the simplicity in which Solomon approached God. He considered all the things which had transpired growing up in a kingdom fraught with violence and war, and he posed a very simple request to God, would You give me wisdom. He knew without it he would never survive, but with it, he could create a kingdom worthy of the One who gave it to him in the first place.

Prayer:
Father, as James said, if any man lacks wisdom let him ask of God, and You will give it liberally. Amen

Day 356

Text:
Dd Today: 2 Sam 22 David understood the power of praise & penned many songs reflecting it. May we be a people whose voices 'sing praises to His name.' ☺

Key Word:
Praise: the offering of grateful homage in words or song, as an act of worship
Synonyms: glorify, exalt, honor

Explanation:
If David, who penned much of the Psalms we have today, understood the power of praise and how it brings the presence of God in such a special and tangible way, shouldn't we embrace and act on this truth each and every day?

Prayer:
We give You praise, oh Lord, for You alone are worthy of our praise. Amen

Day 357

Text:
Dd Today: 2 Cor 2 Thanks be to God who always leads us in triumph in Christ & through us diffuses the fragrance of His knowledge in every place. Awesome! ☺

Key Word:
Fragrance: the quality of being fragrant; a sweet or pleasing scent
Synonyms: balm, smell, aroma, incense, perfume

Explanation:
The knowledge of God is so vast that there is no way we could ever assimilate it, but He chooses to give us bits and pieces small enough so as not to overwhelm us. Yet even small bites sometime feel overwhelming. The one thing that runs true is that knowledge is so sweet and aromatic every time we experience it.

Prayer:
Thank You, Lord, for giving us even the smallest portion of Your knowledge. Amen

Day 358

Text:
Dd Today: 2 Cor 3 To this day, when Moses is read, a veil covers their heart. Nevertheless when one turns to the Lord, the veil is taken away. Access approved! ☺

Key Word:
Veil: something that covers, separates, screens, or conceals
Synonyms: cover, hide, disguise, whitewash, film

Explanation:
I find it very interesting that after Jesus died and the veil in the temple was torn, that the Jews hurriedly went in and repaired it. Some of us get so comfortable being veiled we have trouble letting it go.

Prayer:
Lord, help us to let go once the filter is removed. Amen

Day 359

Text:
Dd Today: Pr 11 The righteousness of the blameless will direct his way aright, the blameless in their ways are His delight. We are to be blameless not sinless. ☺

Key Word:
Blameless: free from or not deserving blame; guiltless
Synonyms: irreproachable, innocent

Explanation:
Many of us have thought that to please God, we had to be sinless and therefore have been frustrated and felt unable to approach Him. Well, I'm here to tell you that isn't the case. He doesn't expect us to be perfect, He very much wants us to

be blameless, coming to Him with our weaknesses and asking forgiveness for our mistakes. He wants relationship.

Prayer:
Lord, help us to realize that You are very much approachable and accept us right where we're at. Amen

Day 360

Text:
Dd Today: 2 Cor 5 For we walk by faith, not by sight. Close your eyes, turn around & take a few steps, open your eyes. Faith's angle is a fresh perspective. ☺

Key Word:
Faith: confidence or trust in a person or thing
Synonyms: hope, tenet, belief, communion

Explanation:
If we just go by the pure physical evidence put before us and nothing else, we will be certain to never get beyond what we see. When Elisha told his servant to look up and asked the Lord to open his eyes, there was a whole spiritual world in operation that he never would have considered had he not had faith.

Prayer:
Lord, help our unbelief. Amen

Day 361

Text:
Dd Today: Pr 13 Those who control their tongue will have a long life; opening your mouth can ruin everything. Putting forth may cause you to be put out. ☺

Key Word:
Ruin: the downfall, decay, or destruction of anything

Synonyms: loss, devastation, rubble, deterioration, torpedo, sink

Explanation:
This is a classic case of not thinking before opening your big mouth. We all at one time or another can be put into this category. And all of us have reaped the consequences of doing just that. Maybe some don't realize it, but they're there.

Prayer:
Lord, please help us to think before we speak. Amen

Day 362

Text:
Dd Today: 1 Kings 3 Solomon loved the Lord & when asked what shall I give you? Give me an understanding heart. May He give us all an understanding heart. ☺

Key Word:
Understanding: To perceive and comprehend the nature and significance of; grasp

Synonyms: know, perspicacity, assimilation

Explanation:
The root of Solomon's request was in his knowing and loving the Lord. The key to our understanding will only come through cultivating a similar relationship with our God.

Prayer:
Wrap Your arms around us and let us feel Your love. Amen

Day 363

Text:
Dd Today: 2 Cor 7 Let us cleanse ourselves from everything that can defile our body or spirit. There is a thing called personal responsibility. Take on yours! ☺

Key Word:
Cleanse: to make clean
Synonyms: scour, restore, sterilize, clean, expurgate

Explanation:
In this day and age, there can't be enough emphasis on taking personal responsibility for our actions. We have long ago slipped into a blame-shifting mentality that creates escapism, always trying to point a finger at someone else. It's high time we point the finger at ourselves first.

Prayer:
Search us, oh God, and know our heart. Amen

Day 364

Text:
Dd Today: Pr 15 Plans go wrong for lack of advice; many advisers bring success. Let your plans be more than plans, plant them in a multitude of counselors. 😊

Key Word:
Lack: something missing or needed
Synonyms: dearth, scarcity, paucity, deficit, insufficiency

Explanation:
There is never an occasion when advice cannot be rendered. It is the occasion when it is not that we get ourselves into trouble. I really appreciate my son in this. He invariably will call when he is in the middle of making a critical decision. He doesn't always take my advice, or does he, no matter, his mind is usually made up, but he just wants to run it by someone he trusts before pulling the trigger.

Prayer:
Lord, help us to be quick to counsel and slow to decide. Amen

Day 365

Text:
Dd Today: 2 Cor 10 But they, measuring themselves by themselves, and comparing themselves among themselves, are not wise. He is our standard not we. 😊

Key Word:
Standard: something considered by an authority or by general consentas a basis of comparison; an approved model
Synonyms: gauge, basis, pattern, guide

Explanation:
I remember when I first began speaking at the little church we started and trying so hard to be like others that I respected in style and delivery. It took me almost a year to realize that God made me who I am and that I had my own style and delivery. It was then that my or His messages took to life and blessed the people.

Prayer:
Lord, help us to see ourselves as You made us. Amen

Wrapping it up

To this day I have continued to send these text messages to my family and a few others who have requested them. They have truly been a blessing and have kept me sane through the many transitions we have recently experienced. I am grateful to God and His word for the inspiration to pen this out, and my only hope is that it does for your family what it continues to do for mine.

My thanks for purchasing this volume, but the key is using it every day to be a blessing to someone else. That is truly where my heart lies.

ADDENDUM

The following passages I have included for reference in case you would like to use them.

Dd Today: Pr 20 Plans succeed through good counsel; don't go to war without wise advice. Hit the floor before you hit the door. ☺

Dd Today: 1 Kings 12 Rehoboam rejected the wise counsel of the elders & listened to his peers. Those who have lived longer than us, often have much wisdom. ☺

Dd Today: 1 Kings 13 Even Jeroboam was healed by the Lord when he cried out to him. If we submit to the Lord He will deliver us, & provide a way of escape. ☺

Dd Today: Pr 25 A person without self-control is like a city with broken-down walls. Control yourself or let the enemy do it. ☺

Dd Today: Gal 5 Stand fast in the liberty by which Christ made us free & do not be entangled again with a yoke of bondage. Leaving behind the old, we are free! ☺

Dd Today: 1 Kgs 16 Most of the kings did evil in the sight of the Lord, but those who humbled themselves found favor. In humility we will find our strength. ☺

Dd Today: 1 Kings 17 It will be that you shall drink from the brook, I have commanded ravens to feed you there. If He tells you to do it, He will make provision. ☺

Dd Today: Eph 2 For we are His workmanship, created in Christ Jesus for good works, which God prepared beforehand that we should walk in them. Go & do good! ☺

Dd Today: 1 Kings 18 Elijah stepped out in faith, 450:1 & God consumed not only the sacrifice, but the 450 as well. When was the last time we stepped out? ☺

Dd Today: Col 2 We were dead, yet now made alive, forgiven, He wiped our slate clean disarming & making a spectacle of principalities. Walk accordingly! ☺

Dd Today: 2 Kings 6 Elisha prayed & the eyes of his servant were opened to see the great host surrounding them. Oh that our eyes would see & our boldness swell. ☺

Dd Today: Pr 12 Anxiety in a man's heart weighs it down, but an encouraging word makes it glad. Anxiety is plentiful, but joy is contagious, create an epidemic. ☺

Dd Today: Pr 13 Hope deferred makes the heart sick, but a dream fulfilled is a tree of life. Joseph was called a dreamer. Dream on and live it! ☺

Dd Today: Pr 14 Those who fear the Lord are secure; He will be a refuge for their children. The foundations for our children's security are laid now, in us. ☺

Dd Today: Pr 15 Plans go wrong for lack of advice; many advisers bring success. The best laid plans can always be tweaked. ☺

Dd Today: Pr 16 Commit your actions to the Lord, and your plans will succeed. Seek first what???? And all these things will be what???? ☺

Dd Today: 1 Thess 5 He who calls you is faithful, who also WILL do or finish it. If you'll let Him!!!! ☺

Dd Today: Pr18 A man's stomach will be satisfied from the fruit of his mouth; From the produce of his lips he shall be filled. What we say really does matter. 😊

Dd Today: Pr 19 27 If you stop listening to instruction, my child, you will turn your back on knowledge. Life is learning & learning is life. 😊

Dd Today: Pr 20 The godly walk with integrity; blessed are their children who follow them. Stick to it there are & will be those watching who need us. 😊

Dd Today: Pr 28 Blessed are those who fear to do wrong, Josiah, heard the law, tore his clothes, & humbled himself. The example of a young man, refreshing. 😊

Dd Today: 2 Tim 2 Nevertheless the solid foundation of God stands, having this seal: The Lord knows those who are His. How's your foundation? Sealed? 😊

Dd Today: Pr 29 The fear of man brings a snare, But whoever trusts in the LORD shall be safe. God is not a respecter of persons, we should be likewise. 😊

Dd Today: 2 Tim 4 I have fought the good fight, I have finished the race, I have kept the faith. Let us fight & finish our race. Above all w/faith. 😊

Dd Today: Pr 4 Take firm hold of instruction, do not let go; Keep her, for she is your life. Learning mode must always be our default setting. 😊

Dd Today: Titus 3 Remind them to be subject to rulers & authorities, obey, be ready for every good work, to speak evil of no one. Hard maybe, necessary yes! 😊

Dd Today: Philemon who once was unprofitable to you, but now is profitable. We have all been like Onesimus, let's follow his example, profitability ahead!! 😊

Dd Today: Pr 7 Keep my commands and live, And my law as the apple of your eye. If we dive into it & swim in it, the word will be a filter in time of need. 😊

Dd Today: Pr 8 Love wisdom, that I may cause those who love me to inherit wealth, that I may fill their treasuries. Walk in wisdom & He Will bless you. ☺

Dd Today: Pr 9 For by me, wisdom, your days will be multiplied and years of life will be added to you. Get wisdom, what do you have to lose? Years!! ☺

Dd Today: Heb 2 For in that He Himself was tempted, He is able to aid those who are tempted. Being tempted, do you think He might be able to help us in ours? ☺

Dd Today: Heb 3 For we have become partakers of Christ if we hold the beginning of our confidence steadfast to the end. Confident obedience! Big word obey. ☺

Dd Today: 1 Chr 5 If we disobey God, He will allow us to be taken into captivity of one form or another. Remember, obedience + a little faith = deliverance ☺

Dd Today: Heb 5 Those who by reason of use have their senses exercised to discern both good and evil. Only by use will our senses become useful. ☺

Dd Today: Heb 6 This hope we have as an anchor of our soul, both sure and steadfast which enters the Presence behind the veil. Solidly anchored or dragging? ☺

Dd Today: Pr 14 Those who fear the Lord are secure; he will be a refuge (a place of trust) for their children. Security & trust, makes me feel warm all over. ☺

Dd Today: Pr 15 A cheerful look brings joy to the heart. Want to make someone's day? Give them a smile, it'll make yours too. ☺ ☺ ☺

Dd Today: Pr 16 Better to be patient than powerful; better to have self-control than to conquer a city. Inner strength will always beat external brawn. ☺

Dd Today: Heb 9 The blood of calves & goats? No! The blood of Christ!! Sweeeet! Nuff said. ☺

Dd Today: Heb 11 Our forefathers looked beyond their circumstances seeing w/eyes of faith. Our hope lies one step beyond what we see, faith takes us there. ☺

Dd Today: Pr 20 Many will say they are loyal friends, but who can find one who is truly reliable? Are you there when trouble begins & when the trouble ends? ☺

Dd Today: Pr 21 If you instruct the wise, they will be all the wiser. When we think we know it all, all is more than we know. ☺

Dd Today: Heb 13 And don't forget to do good and to share with those in need. Forget? How could I forg... OK, I get it!!!

Dd Today: James 1 Humbly accept the word God has planted in your hearts. The longest foot in history is the one between your mind & you heart. ☺

Dd Today: 1 Chron 16:8-36 Read, hear and do as James would say. Thank-to revere or worship with extended hands, the Lord. It is fun to serve the Lord!! ☺

Dd Today: 1 Chron 17 You know your servant. David knew the Lord, the Lord knew David. Do we really know Him? Better yet, does He really know us? ☺

Dd Today: Pr 25 Telling lies about others is as harmful as hitting them with an ax, wounding with a sword, or shooting with a sharp arrow. Go ahead say it now! ☺

Dd Today: James 3 Taming the tongue is a life long project, for what you say will either make the wall thicker or create a door through which to walk. ☺

Dd Today: Pr 28 He who trusts in the Lord will find His devices, he who trusts in himself will find his devices. Your preference? ☺

Dd Today: Pr 29 5 Man is just a man, will always be a man and will always act as a man. The Lord was, is & will be. You can follow Him anywhere and be safe. ☺

Dd Today: 1 Chron 21 Ornan was willing to give all, the place, oxen, implements, wheat, all to David for the Lord. Oh, that we would be as willing as Ornan. ☺

Dd Today: 1 Pet 2 Although He was abused; He never tried to get even. And when He suffered, He made no threats....He did the right thing, shouldn't you? ☺

Dd Today: Pr 1 But whoever listens to Me will dwell safely & will be secure, w/out fear of evil. Listening can prove to be quite beneficial. ☺

Dd Today: Pr 2 All wisdom comes from the Lord, so do common sense and understanding. Common sense, understanding, the difference in good & bad decisions. ☺

Dd Today: Pr 3 My child, use common sense & sound judgment! You will rest without a worry & sleep soundly. You want a good night's sleep? Here ya go!! ☺

Dd Today: 1 Pet 5 And be clothed w/ humility, for God resists the proud, but gives grace to the humble. We put on clothes every day, add one more accessory. ☺

Dd Today: 1 Pet 5 Therefore humble yourselves under the mighty hand of God, that He may exalt you in due time. He thrives on humility, shouldn't we? ☺

Dd Today: Pr 6 For the commandment is a lamp, And the law a light; it is only in darkness we stumble; it is only in light we see. The word is waiting? ☺

Dd Today: Pr 7 And all who were slain by her were strong men. Be careful, for where your are strong often times can become a double weakness. Armor up! ☺

Dd Today: Pr8 For whoever finds me finds life, And obtains favor from the LORD; Bible: $42, reading it: $0, wisdom gained: priceless. ☺

Dd Today: 1 Chr 28 Be strong & of good courage & do it; do not fear nor be dismayed, for the LORD will be with you. He will not leave you nor forsake you. Do It! ☺

Dd Today: 2 Ch 7 Solomon prayed, fire came, consumed the sacrifice, His glory filled the temple. As we pray, His desire is to fill this temple over & over. ☺

Dd Today: Pr18 The first to speak in court sounds right until the cross-examination begins. One sided stories bring passion, hearing both sides brings truth. ☺

Dd Today: 2 Ch 10 Rehoboam rejected the advice of the older men & instead asked the opinion of the young men. Wise counsel may not be easy, but it is, wise! ☺

Dd Today: Pr 20 The godly walk with integrity; blessed are their children who follow them. Remember 2 legs, 1 mouth, we walk twice as much as we talk. ☺

Dd Today: Pr 21 It is a joy for the just to do justice, but it terrifies evildoers. It is good for the good to do good, the bad rage against it. ☺

Dd Today: Pr 22 A sterling reputation is better than striking it rich. We are not responsible for what others think of us, only to not give them a case. ☺

www.ingramcontent.com/pod-product-compliance
Lightning Source LLC
Chambersburg PA
CBHW031946080426
42735CB00007B/280